A Shepherd's Love

HELPING PASTORS & PEOPLE UNDERSTAND,
EMBRACE, AND RESPECT EACH OTHER IN LOVE

PASTOR VANESSA YOUNG

Editing & Design by
Sweet, Sweet Spirit Publishing
Pike Road, Alabama
www.sweetsweetspiritpublishing.com

authorHOUSE®

AuthorHouse™
1663 Liberty Drive
Bloomington, IN 47403
www.authorhouse.com
Phone: 1 (800) 839-8640

Published by AuthorHouse 03/16/2020

ISBN: 978-1-7283-4959-6 (sc)
ISBN: 978-1-7283-4958-9 (e)

Library of Congress Control Number: 2020904381

Print information available on the last page.

Scripture quotations marked NIV are taken from the Holy Bible, New International
Version®. NIV®. Copyright © 1973, 1978, 1984 by International Bible
Society. Used by permission of Zondervan. All rights reserved. [Biblica]

Scripture taken from the New King James Version®. Copyright © 1982
by Thomas Nelson. Used by permission. All rights reserved.

Scripture taken from the NEW AMERICAN STANDARD BIBLE®,
Copyright © 1960,1962,1963,1968,1971,1972,1973,1975,1977,1
995 by The Lockman Foundation. Used by permission

This book is printed on acid-free paper.

DEDICATED WITH THANKS TO

My Husband, Pastor Darrell Young

My Parents Pastor Jerry and
First Lady Betty Bridges

Pastor Norva Ross

Pastor Deena Williams

Sister Maria Gilmore

Shawn Stoval

The Prophetic Company

Our Point of Grace Family

CONTENTS

CONTENTS

INTRODUCTION

WHERE IT ALL BEGAN ...

It began as I was going into my ninth year of answering the call to shepherd God's sheep. I came to the realization that many sheep as well as shepherds have begun this race with good intentions, only to be hurt, confused and sometimes disgusted by misconceptions of what they perceive the church experience should entail. I use the word *entail* loosely (by Webster's definition meaning *to involve (something) as a necessary or inevitable part or consequence*) because over the years, I have observed numerous well-meaning believers as they embark upon the journey of finding a church to call home. He or she commits and makes a covenant to a local assembly only to realize that they have made an agreement where the Holy Spirit was not consulted. The Bible clearly states the Holy Spirit "will lead and guide us into all truth" (John 16:13 NIV).

The truth is that connecting to a local assembly can be one of the most fulfilling, life changing experiences that Believers may have the pleasure of experiencing in their lives. Even though this should be a liberating experience, I have had the displeasure of observing the extreme opposite: feelings of not fitting in and expecting the best only to find out the culture of this body of Believers is not for them.

As a result a dilemma is created, and the gravity of their decision comes full circle. They have made a public commitment that they should not have or that needs to be rescinded. What are they to do? The purpose of this offering is to bring enlightenment to spiritual choices we have made or may be in the process of making concerning connecting to a ministry and calling it home. It is my prayer that this book will help alleviate unnecessary stress for those who are sincerely seeking a sacred place to join with other Believers in praise and worship.

If YOU are at the crossroads of this crucial, life-changing decision, this book is for you. A few variables will be revealed to help aid in your decision-making process. If, through prayer and agreement, you read this book in alignment with its purest intent, you will also gain the necessary tools on how to understand and glean from your shepherd's love language, a building process that is essential in having a harmonious relationship.

CHAPTER 1

---◆◆◆---

HELP, I THINK I JOINED THE WRONG CHURCH!

I would like to begin with an amusing story that may leave you scratching your head and wondering how in the world this could happen? It's a brief story of a wonderful woman who realized she joined the wrong church. Here's a little information about her background. She is one of five children born and reared in Alabama where commitment to attending church was instilled at a very young age. Church was a requirement, not an option.

Upon graduating from college, she followed her dreams and ventured out of her hometown to relocate to Lorain, a small town in Ohio. When she arrived, the city was booming with the steel mills and the auto industries which afforded many families the luxuries of living a so-called "good life." Her brother was already living in Ohio and encouraged her to come and experience this new way of living. She was not only on the hunt for a job, but also for a church where she could be under *"watch care"* - otherwise identified as a spiritual covering. As she reminisced and proceeded to share her story, I took note of her body language. There was a non-verbal expression every time she used the phrase *watch care*. The importance of this type of spiritual covering had been so ingrained in her that she understood the necessity of making the same effort in finding a spiritual home as she had made in finding a natural home.

Watch care was designed for college students, transients,

> *The importance of this type of spiritual covering had been so ingrained in her that she understood the necessity of making the same effort in finding a spiritual home as she had made in finding a natural home.*

and people who were in the process of relocating or in a temporary residency situation. When a person is under watch care, it is clearly understood by all parties involved that the sole purpose of this relationship is to stay connected to the body of Christ which is executed by attending a local place of worship. Attendance is understood to be temporary unless you seek to be released from your former place of worship. That release comes through the individual's desire to formally connect to another assembly. Until a formal release has taken place, the person under watch care understands involvement, while in your transition process, has limitations. One major limitation while under watch care is that you have no voting rights and most churches will not allow you to attend business meetings due to your semi-committed role. Therefore, you will not be privy to the operations of the church.

Watch care is more of a southern tradition because many southerners left their homes in search of a better life and upon leaving, their families would send them away with what little they had. Many times, it was only food and a prayer, with the belief that if you continue to pray you will always have food. Many of the prayer petitions included asking God to help their loved ones find a church home. Though many had minimal material possessions, they understood the ultimate possession was the confidence in knowing they were never alone because they had God. But they had still better hurry and get in a church!

Ann is her name, and she didn't hesitate to begin her search to find this church her brother had been describing. She knew the color. She knew or thought she knew its proximity to where she was currently residing. The only problem was there were two churches in that vicinity that matched the description he gave her. Relying on her brother's description and what she thought were her instincts, she walked through the doors

> *Before the benediction, where it was customary to hear the familiar statement, "the doors of the church are open," something must have hit her. It hit a spiritual nerve or an emotional nerve. Ann rose from her seat and with all eyes on her (at least all eyes except her brother's), she made what seemed like a very long walk down the aisle to the front.*

of one of many churches in that small town. After being greeted by ushers, she was escorted to her seat where she sat down and began to partake in the worship portion of the service.

To be honest, her worship was interrupted, a self-interruption I might add because she was so focused on scanning the room in search of her brother. His lack of attendance did not deter her from staying for the service. This routine continued for weeks. She would walk into the sanctuary, be escorted to her seat by the ushers, then begin to scan the congregation in search of her brother. His absence, according to her, did not deter her from attending, but soon her disappointment turned to confusion. Why was he not here? This was her walk and though she had been guided by her brother, she knew she must walk it alone.

One Sunday there was nothing out of the ordinary concerning the service. Before the benediction, where it was customary to hear the familiar statement, "the doors of the church are open," something must have hit her. It hit a spiritual nerve or an emotional nerve. Ann rose from her seat and with all eyes on her (at least all eyes *except* her brother's), she made what seemed like a very long walk down the aisle to the front. Once there she sat in the chair that had been placed there. Although her brother's eyes were not a part of those that watched her as she traveled down front on that Sunday morning, it really didn't matter. She joined the church. I hope you paid attention to the statement *"something must have hit her."* When I asked what prompted her to make such a serious commitment, she could not explain. We will approach this reoccurring phenomenon later.

Unfortunately, the feelings that overshadowed and prompted her to take that great hall of fame walk to the chair positioned in the front of the church did not last long. Nevertheless she continued to be faithful in her attendance for the usual weekly Bible study. As time grew on, her routine scan of the congregation turned to feelings of concern (not anxiety but concern) about the lack of her brother's presence. A fretful day arrived. Something seemed a little off. The deacons began to pray, she thought "Oh no!" The pastor began his sermon and she thought, *"What did I hear before that made me join this church?"* Her next thoughts were, "Wow, what have I gotten myself into?" Ann's struggle came from the fact that while the people connected to this ministry were warm, friendly, and inviting, she knew she made a mistake.

Later that night, Ann stated that she felt like Jacob and "wrestled all night" (Genesis 32:24). Her wrestling was with her conscience. She felt horrible for many reasons. First, she recognized that she had joined this church out of emotions without revelation. The next reason for her wrestling match was the fact that these were nice people who showed genuine love for her. You can probably guess what the enemy did next. He became an accuser of the brethren and tried his best to release a spirit of condemnation.

To make matters even worse she went to work the following Monday and somehow, while talking to her co-workers, the topic of their conversation turned to the local churches in the area. Coupled with being a young woman and a little naive as to how much to share, she started telling them about her most recent experience. She shared how she had joined a church but now felt she made a mistake. This church where her brother apparently attended but she had yet to see him there. Before she could engage her co-workers into more of this intriguing story, out of nowhere a pain hit her

> *First, she recognized that she had joined this church out of emotions without revelation.*
>
> *The next reason for her wrestling match was the fact that these were nice people who showed genuine love for her.*

leg. Her co-worker who would later become her sister-in-law, kicked her under the table and made a "zip those lips" gesture. She obliged and shut her mouth. No one had to shout or kick her again. Her future sister-in-law spared her the humiliation of talking about the home church of her coworkers' family. When I say family, I'm not saying that the father is the pastor, but a large majority of her coworker's family attended and the deacon that she was getting ready to discuss was her co-worker's brother. That is what we would call a "family church." We will discuss that later. She got the hint and a bruise.

Ann finally called her brother and relayed what had become her weekly concern. "Why haven't you been going to church? You know better than that!" His response baffled her. He said, "I have been at church every Sunday as well as Bible study." Then he asked the question, "**What church have you been attending**?" When she told him the name of the church, he informed her he was at the church down the street. I was shocked, amused and somewhat surprised that it took her so long to find out where he had been going. If it had been me, after the first Sunday of me thinking that my brother was a no show, I would have made every effort to find out why! I asked what she did next.

Her quick response was, "I left that church and started attending his." I go back to what my mother has always stated, "Everything in life is a learning tool followed by the question: what did you learn from that?" Ann's response to the question was "the things you have been taught in your childhood may need to be explored more closely when you reach adulthood."

I now repeat my mother's question, "What have I learned?" from Ann's story. I learned that faith cometh by hearing and true enough, having a covering is vital for one's continual spiritual growth. Proverbs 4:7 NIV says, "Wisdom is the principal thing, therefore get wisdom: and with all thy getting get understanding." What did Ann miss to make her join a church and then be overcome with such weighty regret? The truth is that Ann's story is not unusual in the body of Christ. Admonishing someone to be obedient without wisdom can lead to heartache, frustration, and confusion. Ann made it out without being wounded or feeling like a betrayer but that is not the case for many believers. If you are at the crossroads of making the decision to stay or leave a ministry, it is crucial that you pay attention to a few warnings that I have for you:

1. **Check your emotions**. When making such crucial decisions, especially if your emotions are raging like a roller coaster, STOP BEFORE GOING FORWARD. Seek alone time with the Holy Spirit and let Him speak to you. A prime example of this is Jesus being led by the Holy Spirit into the wilderness (Matthew 4 & Luke 4). While there, He was forced to confront his humanity as our Savior in the fulfilling of His purpose as our kinsmen redeemer. Scripture details how the enemy was relentless in pursuing his goal of trying to cancel Jesus' assignment and cause the Perfect Will of God to be aborted. Jesus demonstrated how we can take authority over our emotions if we depend on the Word. Satan is an accuser and enticer, yet in this situation, he forgot one thing: he was conversing with the Word. John 1:1 states "In the beginning was the Word, and the Word was with God, and the Word was God."

In your decision-making process it is crucial that you fast and find scripture to aid you toward the path that is correct for YOU. If Jesus didn't know that He was the Word, then He would not have been able to withstand and defeat the enemy. When the enemy tried to tempt Jesus into throwing himself off the pinnacle (a place where the Holy Spirit had taken Him), His response was not driven by fleshly influences. He had every right to respond by saying, "Do you know who I am?" Instead, His response showed that The Savior remained emotionally stable and intact. He said, "It is written." The Word spoke the Word. I encourage you to imitate Jesus' example. Check your emotions and find confirming scriptures to cling to during your decision-making process. This is of utmost importance at this stage of the process.

2. **Subdue your natural senses**. We have five senses: sight, hearing, touch, taste, smell. It has been proven that when someone loses one sense, the others become stronger. This is true in the natural realm. The body kicks into gear and compensates for any deficiency. It is a natural phenomenon for which man cannot take credit. As believers, we are not supposed to base our life's decisions on natural occurrences, but we are instructed to filter them through the Holy Spirit (I John 4:1). The natural begins to perish at the moment we enter the world, therefore our survival requires us to be Kingdom minded. When a Kingdom mind is not activated, Believers find themselves falling into pits

under the assumption they were properly discerning the atmosphere when actually they were operating in their natural senses.

Let's look at a few scenarios connected to our sense of sight. Perhaps someone observes the actions of another and instead of petitioning the Holy Spirit for clarity, they start to form conclusions based on their natural observations – or what they see with their natural eyes. Humans are generally creatures of habit. We are generally moved by the aesthetics of our environment. The saying is that "beauty is in the eyes of the beholder" and our perceptions of beauty (or what brings pleasure through the eye-gate) usually plays a role in the acceptance or denial of a person, place or thing.

The word of God reveals that man's choice is not always God's choice. When Samuel set out on his assignment to look for Saul's replacement, Jesse paraded his sons before the prophet knowing that a king was in the midst. Son after son came and went and somehow there was no king chosen. David, the young shepherd boy never crossed his father's mind, yet he was always on God's heart. *"But the Lord said to Samuel, 'Do not consider his appearance or his height for I have rejected him. The Lord does not look at the things man does. Man looks at the outward appearance, but the Lord looks at the heart"* (I Samuel 16:7 NIV). David was anointed to be the next king of Israel and later asked himself, *"What is man, that thou art mindful of him? And the son of man, that thou visitest him?"* (Psalm 8:4 NIV).

Our sense of hearing can also be a strong motivator in how we process thoughts and make decisions. Natural hearing deals with natural discernment which is usually based on experiences that are common to people. These are experiences that we don't have to petition the Holy Spirit for because we have already dealt with them at some point in our natural life. In many of my prophetic teachings I expound on experiential knowledge where some may say they received a prophetic word. Actually what was released were **words of knowledge** that came from experiences in life. This can be placed in the category of perception.

There is something called spiritual perception. Nehemiah 6:12 reads, "Then I *perceived* that surely God had not sent him, but he uttered his prophecy against me because Tobiah and Sanballat had hired him." When Nehemiah and the returning remnant were nearing the completion of rebuilding the wall, false prophets were sent to bring fear. The words they heard caused them to sin because they did not believe the report of the Lord. When we spiritually perceive, we cannot always say that God or the Holy Spirit has revealed it to us. Our past experiences play a significant revelatory role when coupled with the Holy Spirit. The Holy Spirit will then give us the confirmation that what we are receiving is correct.

Spiritual hearing may not be an audible voice, although it is possible. If a clear answer or directive doesn't arrive after you have petitioned God with pure motives for clarity, then continue in your last place of obedience to His voice. **Remember, the teacher is silent when the student is taking the test.** As Kingdom-dwellers, we understand protocol and authority that comes with our birthright. Having received that birthright through Christ Jesus, we also understand that being tossed to and fro is unacceptable! We cannot be tossed when we operate within the spirit realm. This will, however, only take place when we subdue the natural man which means bringing under control anything that alters our God ordained destiny.

3. **Consult the Holy Spirit**. The personhood of the Holy Spirit that resides in all Believers will help guide you in your decision-making process. Many Believers consult - or should I say solicit - opinions from others. Well-meaning as they may be, they forget the access they have to the will of the Father residing in them. I will never underestimate the value of sound counsel but that must come after conversations (prayers) with the Father. Proverbs 11:14 warns that "where there is no counsel, the people fall; but in the multitude of counselors there is safety." This passage of scripture confirms that seeking guidance from elders and those who have already traveled the path we are on is not only wise but can also provide safety.

I have asked individuals if they sought guidance from anyone concerning their current position, the overwhelming response time and time again is "Yes!" My next question is, "Have you been totally fair in how you perceived and presented your situation to those from whom you have received counsel?" I ask this follow-up question because I understand that we will not get Godly counsel if we are carnal in our presentation of the situation. It is a natural human tendency to present our case in a way that benefits us. But true wisdom must be connected to honesty. Facts, not emotions, are necessary for the will of God to manifest and for us to get the best results.

4. **Respond to the direction that you have received.** If you have taken all the other steps, this one is usually the hardest: do what you have been told. "Faith without works is dead" (James 2:20, 26 NKJV). Faith, though unseen, can be felt when you are in the will of the Father. Being in the will of the Father may not be the most popular thing in other's eyes, but this is personal. Some things do not require an explanation or justification.

> 1. Check your emotions.
> 2. Subdue your natural senses.
> 3. Consult the Holy Spirit.
> 4. Respond to the direction that you have received.

CHAPTER 2

———◆·◆·◆———

IN GREEN PASTURES: UNDERSTANDING CULTURES

Every place of worship has its own culture. The world labels it as "style of worship," but the truth is these are cultures – some of which are created without realizing it. Culture in a place of worship is not based on the nationality of the congregants but rather on the attitudes and behavioral characteristics of that particular social group. This means that a church may have the same physical characteristics as the place of worship down the street, but how each culture worships, interacts with, and approaches Abba Father is unique to each. Yet they remain in the same spiritual family, brothers and sisters in Christ. In our biological families we can attest to having siblings that we have glibly questioned, "Where in the world did *they* come from?" Posing the question doesn't exclude them from the family – just as their actions don't.

Culture can be observed and felt when we are new in the faith or spiritually immature because our initial observation is

> *Culture in a place of worship is not based on the nationality of the congregants but rather on the attitudes and behavioral characteristics of that particular social group.*

often with our natural senses. That is excusable in our infantile spiritual state, but as we mature in Christ, we must observe through discernment. I have come to believe that many believers lack this fundamental gift and if they would only ask, it would be freely given. "If any of you lack wisdom," James 1:5 instructs us, "let him ask of God, that giveth to all men liberally, and upbraideth not; and it shall be given him." This inevitably would assist us in avoiding many misconceptions, heartaches and challenges that come from the guessing game so many people play.

Your decision as to your place of worship should not, simply cannot be like rolling dice where one calls out what they believe they should receive based on physical observations and odds. You should never say, "I only have four choices so let me take a chance." I cannot count how many times I sat in my office and looked across the desk at well-meaning brothers and sisters who came seeking spiritual guidance in finding a place of worship or clarity regarding the place that they may be currently attending. I *intentionally never tell* anyone where they should go. My level of authority is only to direct them to rely upon the Holy Spirit since He said He would guide us into all truths. Instead, I do my best to enlighten them to the truth about matters which may be out of our control and encourage them not to bring old issues into the new covenant relationship.

WHAT ARE SOME THINGS THAT ARE BEYOND OUR CONTROL BUT MIGHT INFLUENCE CULTURES?

- Biological families - We cannot change our natural DNA or ethnicity. Other physical features that can only be altered through the means of surgery or strenuous exercise. In the spiritual arena, upon acceptance of Jesus Christ as our personal Lord and Savior, our family lineage changes from children of the devil to children of God.

- Economic limitations – The world's economy can sometimes affect the Believer which is one of the reasons the Bible instructs us to pray for our government. Poor decision-making on our part can also affect us in a variety of ways. Luke 14:28 reads, "For which of you, desiring to build a tower, does not first sit down and count the cost, whether he has enough to complete it?"

- Vocations - At times people settle for jobs which they may not particularly enjoy but the benefits outweigh enjoyment or pay. While changing jobs might be within their control, doing so would negatively impact their current lifestyle (financial obligations, community connections, family).

The last two scenarios are the only ones that can change with God, hard work and a determined spirit. Nevertheless, I still encounter many believers that feel pressure in their decision-making process because of the affect they feel it will have on others.

In order to discern the culture of a church you must **PAY ATTENTION** to everything! Do not judge or criticize the created atmosphere and structure of the church. Cultures in places of worship may be formed with or without it being intentional but over time and repetition, cultures are set. Even in our natural house we have set cultures. Some can remember their mom say, "What we do in this house stays in this house!" What was really being said was this is our culture, and if you don't like it then you don't have to come over.

In my mother's house it was instilled that you don't go anywhere unannounced or uninvited. As a young girl, I can recall people knocking at our front door and my mother's response was always the same: "Don't you open that door." At first, we didn't understand and almost felt like it was unfair to those who made the trip to our house. Now as an adult I realize it was the culture that had been set in our house. Cultures have nothing to do with being fair. They are merely the established standard.

Cultures can be passed down through generations as they become the norm for those who have adhered to them. Perhaps you've heard the illustration of the woman who would cut off the ends of her

> *Do not judge or criticize the created atmosphere and structure of the church. Cultures in places of worship may be formed with or without it being intentional but over time and repetition, cultures are set.*

roast before she cooked it. When asked by her family why she would do this, her response was that it was how her mother cooked her roasts. At some point, she became curious about her own actions and called her mother to inquire about this tradition. "Mom, why did you cut off the ends of your roast before you cooked it?" Her mother said, "Because I didn't have a pan big enough to hold it."

Her mother had set a culture without realizing it. That culture would later be passed on without explanation or understanding of why it existed. That is an example of a harmless culture. **But some cultures can cause delays in our lives or affect others in negative ways. I would say these type of set cultures can be broken but first must be acknowledged.** All churches have their own culture and unless you are in leadership or a part of the majority that holds power in that culture, you generally will not have the ability to change the culture. I want to offer one more discussion about personal cultures. Prayerfully, this will further aid you in understanding church cultures.

The Generational Culture Trap

You may be familiar with a television program called "Super Nanny." It is centered around the experiences of a professional nanny who comes to live with families needing intervention. Yes, they were in crisis, but not the kind of crisis you might expect. Somehow the children in the family have become so out of control that the parents were crying for help. So much so that they enlist the help of Super Nanny. I'm telling you, she must have a cape on underneath her long dresses because some of those kids are a hot mess!

The nanny, upon observation and through discussion with the parents, assists them in setting goals. Often the goals are to develop a sense of respect, structure and discipline that hopefully will be carried on long after her departure. I have asked my husband, "What do you think she would say about our home?" I really would love her to come and assess our home. Not because we have disrespectful children. On the contrary, the Lord has truly blessed my husband and I with two wonderful young men. Here's why I asked.

Being a busy salon owner for over twenty-eight years, my hours fluctuate weekly. It didn't help having a husband who worked rotating shifts. I thank God that we were blessed to have two mothers who took turns watching our boys. Everybody's schedule revolved around ours so that meant there appeared to be no set structure. The culture in our home was a lot of hustle and bustle, fueled by rushed hectic mornings of trying our best to be on time for school. We struggled with punctuality because of the many late-night hours at the salon. It was not uncommon for me to call my mother and say, "Don't worry about waking the boys. We will spend the night."

My wonderful mother would have them fed and in the bed, so all I would have to do is crawl in next to them. My wonderful mother-in-law, on the other hand, would have them sparkling clean because her love language was bath time. Both mothers had them in the bed, but one fed them and the other bathed them. Both showed love and support, yet

> *Often the goals are to develop a sense of respect, structure and discipline that hopefully will be carried on long after her departure. I have asked my husband, "What do you think she would say about our home?"*

they created distinct personal cultures. I've often wondered what Super Nanny would say about my husband and I working so much and shuffling our sons from home to home. Would it be something like, "You are well-meaning parents, but have created too little structure for your children"? Or would she ask, "Is this is a learned behavior and if so, where did it come from?"

I grew up watching my mother work on projects until the last minute. By the grace of God she would always make it happen! So, using my sense of sight I never saw her fail in getting things accomplished, and it was always done with excellence I might add. Success was connected to hurriedness even if it brought on anxiousness. But God doesn't want His children to be anxious for anything (Philippians 4:6). As a child I labeled it as tardiness, but as an adult I must call it for what it is: procrastination (the action of delaying or postponing something).

I never viewed her actions as postponing her tasks. I felt all the hats she wore interfered with her schedule. So many mothers wear the hats of wife, nurturer, taxi driver, banker, coach, and so on. Truth is, even though my father was in the house, my mother also wore the spiritual leader hat in our home. Not because she wanted to but because my father chose not to. After every accomplished task I would hear her make the proclamation, "I am not going to wait this long next time!" But next time came, and she played the waiting game AGAIN only to come out on the winner's side AGAIN. I followed in her footsteps and continued in the culture of procrastination, but what I have learned didn't stop in her home. I have continued to carry this legacy, and sad to say, I'm just now acknowledging its hold on my life.

After my formative years, I followed the Word of the Lord and was not unequally yoked. I married into a family where my future mother-in-love was a phenomenal seamstress who did some of her best work at the last minute. This looked familiar to me. Anyone that knew her can attest to her smiling and giggling only to say to her customers, "Please take a seat while I finish." So procrastination has constantly surrounded me. I could not seem to get out of its clutches. More importantly, no one told me not to get my children caught up in its binding grip.

> *I followed in her footsteps and continued in the culture of procrastination, but what I have learned didn't stop in her home. I have continued to carry this legacy, and sad to say, I'm just now acknowledging its hold on my life. I married into a family where my future mother-in-love was a phenomenal seamstress who did some of her best work at the last minute.*

This is a **generational culture trap** that I have not yet broken. Why? Because generational issues – sometimes referred to as generational curses - are usually deemed to be dark and sinister in nature. The truth is a generational issue is **anything** that has been passed down generationally. This is a textbook example that I must admit still has not been broken. I am having the scales removed off my eyes even as I am writing this book.

CHAPTER 3

———◆◆———

HE LEADETH ME: THE PROCESS OF TRUTH

In the process of writing this book, so many memories started flooding my mind. I can recall events that were part of my children's daily routine that should not have been. When my boys were in the fourth and fifth grade, we would be in such a rush to beat the late bell for school, that they understood what to do when they saw this certain stop sign. They were instructed to unfasten their seat belts and get ready to jump out and run into the building to make it before the bell would ring! This was such the norm in our daily routine that I didn't even have to tell them: it became common.

Sidebar: familiarity can only be called such when we create a common relationship with it, the situation, the person, the circumstance, etc. Now I realize I must break over my sons' lives the familiarity (or comfort) of living a life of procrastination. It can cause them nothing but anxiousness and even health issues and other misdiagnosed problems. My mother's cultural habit of procrastination became my cultural habit and now my sons are susceptible to this vicious cycle.

But Thanks be to God! The blessed truth is that the cycle can be ended if someone breaks its hold. I realized my actions didn't necessarily cause outward issues, but inwardly my sons were becoming familiar with something that would do them no good in the long run. That's how familiar spirits operate as well. They appear innocent until we pause to examine their hidden intentions, often due to the prompting of the Holy Spirit. I searched my memory bank and the Holy Spirit revealed how strong this generational hold happened to be.

> *Sidebar: familiarity can only be called such when we create a common relationship with it, the situation, the person, the circumstance, etc. Now I realize I must break over my sons' lives the familiarity (or comfort) of living a life of procrastination. It can cause them nothing but anxiousness and even health issues and other undiagnosed problems. My mother's cultural habit of procrastination became my cultural habit and now my sons are susceptible to this vicious cycle.*

On the days when we just happened to be on time, which were few and far in between, I would hear the usual click of the seat belts unfastening even though they were on time. The culture was set that we were running behind. The first time I noticed this happen it broke my heart and I said, "Tomorrow I will do better." That lasted about one week, and we were back to our culture, run, move, and make it just in the nick of time.

When I look back, I can remember my mother working about five miles from home, but her daily routine was to take her rollers out of her hair and put her makeup on in the car. I can even recall her being a Sunday school teacher. We would come running into church Sunday after Sunday just in time! Mind you she was never late, but right on time. She would drop her bags and teach a great class. But because she was there "on time," no one knew what it took or what we went through to get there. Since my mother was big on respect, we respected others time just not our own. When you understand culture, you create your own culture based upon the culture that created you. You will have a greater comprehension of the cultures you gravitate toward.

Before we go any farther, I ask you to be honest with yourself. Think. Have you created a familiar culture personally or for others in your family which may not be healthy? What are the habits, actions, conversations, and ways of interacting with others have been modeled before your children that might be absolutely detrimental to them as they mature? Even in the ministry family of which you are a part, are there cultural habits that threaten to weaken the very fabric of the ministry? Is there anything you can do to turn the tide toward a healthier cultural status quo? If so, please take a moment to repent if necessary and pray for God's guidance so that future generations won't have to battle their predecessors' creations.

You may actually be living in the culture you did not create but want to get out of and be released from once and for all. In order to do so, you must confess the negative culture and forgive those that created it. Then you will be positioned to break its grip on your life and cancel its assignment for the generations that will come after you. Next, you need to decree that you are no longer under bondage. Decree this scripture and say this sample prayer:

If the Son makes (me) free, (I) SHALL be
free indeed (John 8:36 NKJV)

Most Gracious and Heavenly Father, I come before you asking
you to forgive me for creating a culture of (you fill in the
blank). I repent from that way of thinking, living, and today
I decree and declare that my mind shall follow Your lead.
I Thank You that You said in 1 John 1:9 "If we confess
our sins, You are faithful and just to forgive us our
sins and to cleanse us from all unrighteousness."
Father, today don't let my former actions hinder
me or those that are connected to me.
I receive a new culture that You have ordained
before the foundation of the world.
In Jesus Name, I seal this prayer in the blood
of the Lamb. Amen. Amen. Amen.

CHAPTER 4

———◆◆◆———

HE RESTORES MY SOUL: TYPES OF CHURCH CULTURES

I want to present nine (9) types of church cultures – although the list could go on and on due to the possible combination of these cultures as well as those I do not explore here. The ones we'll touch on here are:

1. Music/Worship-Based Culture
2. Word-based Culture
3. Charismatic Culture
4. Contemporary Culture
5. Traditional Culture
6. Networking Culture
7. Community-Focused Culture
8. Seeker-Friendly Culture
9. Prophetic Culture

1. Music/Worship-Based Culture is developed around and based on the music in the church. Sad to say sometimes it is just music - and not worship. A mature Christian can often discern the difference. When the congregants only participate during specific songs, that is music-based worship. If participation is based around the sound of worship, the specificity of the song does not matter. The response of the congregants to the spiritual move in the atmosphere, not the song title, sets the service for healing, deliverance and the preached Word. In an atmosphere that is set by worship, people will not have the ability to stifle the front-line worshippers because they have positioned themselves on the walls to hear the Song of the Lord for the house. This Song might not even be anything that was rehearsed by the praise team or that has ever been heard before. It is the clarion call from the Holy Spirit that serves as an invitation to enter into God's Presence during the collective worship experience. You will notice most leaders in this type of culture have some musical background and they are usually worshippers themselves. If this is not the culture for you, you may see yourself in another group we're going to explore.

There are people who purposely miss the praise and worship part of the service because they may feel it is too long or unnecessary for them to get into the presence of the Lord. These are individuals who probably don't belong in the music/worship-based

> *If participation is based around the sound of worship, the specificity of the song does not matter. The response of the congregants to the spiritual move in the atmosphere, not the song title, sets the service for healing, deliverance and the preached Word.*

culture. They have timed when the praise and worship will end, and they arrive in time for the Word. People who are not designed for the music/worship-based culture often watch the clock and count the songs until the Word is delivered. This group could be in the presence of the most gifted psalmist but cannot discern that their worship is not contained in song. We must remember worship is not always achieved through music. *However, a music/worship atmosphere is not only important in this culture, it is the lifeline of the ministry. This culture beats to the drums of the Spirit of God.* The music/worship-based culture understands that the sound of the Lord is vital for leading others from the outer court to the inner court, God's Holy Place, through worship. This culture can touch heaven through sound with or without words.

2. Word-based Culture is formed around the written Word of God. Here is a group of people who are drawn to the teaching aspect of church. They may also usually like the good old-fashioned preachers. So put those two anointings together, and you have what I call "teachers." They truly believe the Word is the most important aspect of their culture and if you get any of the other elements, you are getting a bonus. I've heard the Word culture preacher say, "No praise and worship today. Let's just get into the Word." People that are drawn to the Word culture can handle the fluff, but they will overload on too many incidentals.

This group, when asked what the sermon was about, will be able to give you the scripture reference, topic and sub-topic. This congregant engages in service by taking notes and during the week dive into additional research regarding what was spoken about. This culture values the historical contents of the Word. The underside of this group at times may be so analytical that if they receive too many other elements during a worship service, it will cause them to miss out on the spiritual interpretation. This also at times may cause them to wrestle with head knowledge above faith knowledge. So a teacher can just give them the meat or depth of the Word. They don't want to have to spit out the bones because it does not interest them in the least. As a matter of fact, smoke and lights will generally cause them to question the authenticity of that place of worship. This culture is great for those that are spiritually hungry. I would suggest new converts venture out and seek this culture to help accelerate their spiritual growth. But try to make sure the teaching is Word-based and avoids bias.

> *The underside of this group at times may be so analytical that if they receive too many other elements during a worship service, it will cause them to miss out on the spiritual interpretation. This also at times may cause them to wrestle with head knowledge above faith knowledge.*

3. Charismatic Culture is built on the concept of *charismata* and deals with the operations of the gifts of the Holy Spirit as specified in 1 Corinthians 12:7-11 NKJV.

⁷ But the manifestation of the Spirit is given to every man to profit withal.

⁸ For to one is given by the Spirit the word of wisdom; to another the word of knowledge by the same Spirit;

⁹ To another faith by the same Spirit; to another the gifts of healing by the same Spirit;

¹⁰ To another the working of miracles; to another prophecy; to another discerning of spirits; to another divers kinds of tongues; to another the interpretation of tongues:

¹¹ But all these worketh that one and the selfsame Spirit, dividing to every man severally as he will.

Being drawn to a culture like this generally requires belief in five-fold ministry which includes apostle, prophet, evangelist, pastor and teacher. Many believers have the mindset that two of the five gifts, prophets and apostles, no longer function in the current dispensation. I beg to differ especially when reading the writings of the Apostle Paul in the New Testament. In Isaiah's writings, he made the statement in several places that the Messiah, who was also a prophet, would come to save the lost. Pay attention - Isaiah said, *"He was to come."* The world would accept the last three gifts (evangelist, pastor, teacher) that God gave to the church. I have come to understand why people may struggle with accepting the first two (apostle and prophet). The misuse of these God-given gifts has tainted their function and carries controversy. I understand, and in their defense, I pray that the stigma changes as more of us execute the office with Godly integrity.

In the charismatic culture, you might see the manifestation of the gift of tongues, the working of miracles as well as signs and wonders. This type of culture will not be appealing to those that say, "It doesn't take all that!" Yes, there needs to be order in the house of worship because God does things decently and in order. Signs and wonders, however, are not for the spectators but participators. If a

> *I have come to understand why people may struggle with accepting the first two (apostle and prophet). The misuse of these God-given gifts has tainted their function and carries controversy.*

culture like this is appealing to you, you will find yourself seeking the manifestation not just conversations about the impossible. This type of culture may seem high strung in comparison to the Word culture. This is by no means inferring that the Word is absent from this culture. You will experience the reverence and dependence on the Holy Spirit which is intrinsically apparent in this culture. One must develop a relationship to the third person of the Trinity (i.e., the Holy Spirit) to be comfortable here.

4. **Contemporary Culture** worshippers will drop momma and them off at their desired Word-based or other culture place of worship, but rarely go in themselves. I have even seen them go in speak to the mothers and not see them again until it is time to return to pick up their precious cargo. They will respect that *this* church is for you, but they are seeking relevancy in their language. It does not mean the preacher isn't relevant. What it implies is that your vocabulary has to appeal to their academic and/or street senses.

This group is comprised mostly of the millennials who will Goggle while the preacher is upfront giving his or her all. Fact checking is a way of life for them because from their birth, they have had information at their fingertips. The millennial demographic includes: the college graduates, the accept- my-lifestyle-group, the "governmental college graduates" (the ones who are told that daddy is away at "college" for three to five years but is really incarcerated).

The contemporary group doesn't have to walk a mile in their brother's shoes to stand up and be an advocate for their brother. Their cause is more important than their exposure. These individuals have learned to accept each other's lifestyles, and it is apparent they are learning

> *They will respect that this church is for you, but they are seeking relevancy in their language. It does not mean the preacher isn't relevant. What it implies is that your vocabulary has to appeal to their academic and/or street senses.*

each other's language. I'm by no means saying they agree with each other all the time, but they are tolerant because they desire tolerance. They accept that their predecessors don't understand them, but they want respect. Respect to them is hearing their point of view regardless of whether you agree or not.

The contemporary culture is not concerned with hearing your story every time the doors open. Point them to their Exodus. In their spirit what worked for you probably won't work for them. Many baby boomers will say "He is the same God yesterday, today, and forever more" (Hebrews 13:8 NIV). While this may be fact, the contemporary culture needs more. The contemporary culture has not come to grips with the fact that each generation has been sheltered from storms their parents endured, which cleared paths for their generation to proceed with less of a fight. This type of culture cannot relate to hymns and prefer not to pick up a book to sing a chorus then three stanzas of a song. They don't mind looking at a screen to follow words but holding a paper is unacceptable. This group doesn't want announcements read by sister-so-and-so every time the church door opens. They can read for themselves.

The contemporary style Believer is time conscience. Their stance is, get me to my seat and let me participate in what is comfortable to me. Translation - please don't keep saying "raise your hands" and "tell your neighbor." If your message speaks to this style of Believer, they will tell their friends in their own ways, whether they tweet, record on Facebook or drop nuggets around the water cooler. We must not get this group confused with the seeker-friendly culture. Although they may have many similarities, they also have strong differences.

5. **Traditional Culture** is not to be confused with a religious culture. Religious culture is based on control, manipulation and at times intimidation. It is not uncommon for larger ministries to offer traditional and contemporary style services to accommodate the different worship preferences. In developing striving ministries, pastors are paying close attention to the many generations that may cross their threshold. Many baby boomers prefer the traditional culture, meaning they prefer to continue to use what has worked in the past. Thus their style is more formal and sometimes contains a lot of protocols.

In traditional culture the hierarchy is clear, though it may not be the pastor. It could instead be the deacons, trustees or some sort of board. A perceived benefit of being in this type of culture is noting that change does not happen without voting or advance notice. Many people that are connected to this type of culture like the intimate personal feelings of knowing the names of the sick and shut- in and the use of hymnals. This culture often prefers that the pastor stand at the back of the church after service and shake the hands of all who have come to worship. This personal contact may not be possible with larger congregations, but the atmosphere is more intimate which is the inclination of this culture. You will notice in ministries that offer both traditional and contemporary services, the traditional will always be the first service offered.

6. **Networking Culture** creates an atmosphere that appeals to the believer who prefers the marriage of social and spiritual. Their ideal place of worship is comprised of friends, family and peers who connect through a sense of belonging. In this culture you will find people that not only see themselves as brothers and sisters in the Lord, but who will also interact socially with dinners after service or bonding that leads to the sharing of other interests.

> *In traditional culture the hierarchy is clear, though it may not be the pastor. It could instead be the deacons, trustees or some sort of board. A perceived benefit of being in this type of culture is noting that change does not happen without voting or advance notice.*

In the networking culture you may see business cards being passed out after service because again, social engagement is encouraged and supported in this type of culture. I've witnessed members recommending other members for jobs, giving the best references, and becoming spiritual aunts and uncles. It is where natural DNA takes a back seat to spiritual. This type of culture is surely not void of Word and worship, but it definitely lends its strength to being beneficial to a chosen circle. I find people connect to this type of culture because they have a gift that can be used in the ministry and being connected by a covenant relationship is their way of sowing into the ministry. The notion of giving your time, talents and tithe to ministry is a calling card to many who may not want the world to get all the gifts the Lord has entrusted to them. People in this type of culture are not at all void of desiring an intimate relationship with the Lord, but the perks of connecting outside the four walls of the church are just as important.

7. **Community-focused Culture** is a ministry that will be visible in community affairs whether through food pantries, shelters, governmental organizations, or after school programs. The community minded culture measures itself by the impact it has on the community, not by the size of the congregation. This type of culture will attract extroverts who thrive on one-on-one interaction. Passion is evident in this type of culture.

The community-focused culture seeks to fulfill the needs of the community. Sometimes the needs are revealed by members who were at one time in need themselves. They join this type of culture to give back. It is the pay-it-forward type of culture for some and volunteering is valued. The other group of people in this culture recognize how blessed they are by God, so they desire to give in proportion to what they have received. This is the prime example of blessed to be a blessing.

This culture will appeal to the one who doesn't mind getting up early, working late, and maybe never getting a thank you. Their thanks come from seeing the needs fulfilled. Members thrive on seeing the physical, emotional and social economic needs met in their local assembly, and their help will extend beyond their personal connections. This culture will help the ministry down the street and expect nothing in return. I have observed many in this culture who are connected to community and civic organizations.

If you are called to social action or the holistic needs of individuals the community minded culture is for you. The spiritual component as recorded in James 2:17 NKJV gives us insight into this culture. *"So also faith by itself, if it does not have works, is dead."* You will receive relevant sermons

> *The community-focused culture seeks to fulfill the needs of the community. Sometimes the needs are revealed by members who were at one time in need themselves. They join this type of culture to give back.*

with sweat equity. The teaching will be seen in the action of their leaders. Life beyond Sunday is real. This culture equips strong missionary workers for their tasks at hand.

Finally, those drawn to the community culture are likely endowed with the spirit of the Good Samaritan. The tenet of being their brother's keeper drives them with the understanding that your brother may not look, sound, or act like them. But in showing the passion of Christ, they can fulfill the desire to be like Christ themselves.

8. **Seeker-Friendly Culture** is easy to define on the surface but is a little deeper than what may appear. Webster's defines seeking as "the attempt to find something." Whenever I have

engaged in conversation with someone who is associated with a seeker-friendly culture, I realize it is not that the seeker doesn't want the Word, music and networking. As a matter of fact all those cultures appeal to them! Truth is the seeker friendly wants all those cultures just without all the structure and rules of someone saying, "You have to join to belong." Their thinking is "If I come, isn't that good enough? My commitment is apparent by my presence." People in this type of culture may come to a church for months even years without joining or formally committing to the ministry. I've even known people who have attended churches for years, served in ministry, and sown financially . . . but committing in the traditional sense doesn't always happen in this type of culture.

Let me tell you of a funny story that happened to me. Anyone who knows me knows I love resale shopping. One day while getting my retail therapy, I was in a shop and this woman approached me and asked me which dress I liked. I chose this colorful floral print dress. She agreed and so I asked her where she planned on wearing it. "To my church," she responded. So because I am a Pastor, I asked a natural question. "What church?" She responded without hesitation - "Point of Grace." That just happened to be the church where my husband and I pastored. I almost said, "I heard they have awesome pastors." You may ask why she didn't recognize me? I am also a licensed cosmetologist and I change my hairstyle frequently. The pulpit look is not like the retail therapy look!

I soon concluded that she had visited a few times and it was apparent she wasn't attending any other place, but the seeker friendly side of her was drawn to Point of Grace - just not enough to join. You will find that people in this type of culture claim a ministry that is appealing to them without having to be written on the roll. This culture appeals to those who want to connect spiritually, but that's where it ends. They are particular about who is invited into their personal space. They will let you know if or when you can have access to more of it and perhaps a deeper relationship.

> *My commitment is apparent by my presence." People in this type of culture may come to a church for months even years without joining or formally committing to the ministry. I've even known people who have attended churches for years, served in ministry, and sown financially . . . but committing in the traditional sense doesn't always happen in this type of culture.*

Of all the cultures mentioned, the seeker-friendly and the contemporary are the most similar in that most who are drawn to these primarily want one thing: **to be accepted**. The major difference is that the seeker friendly can be hypersensitive about getting their needs met without acknowledging the fact that places of worship survive and are run by the body. Therefore, without them being committed to the body, it will not properly function in its God ordained purpose. Seeker friendly individuals can sometimes look more at the wrapping on the gift box rather than the gift that is inside. I have encountered people who are drawn to the seeker friendly culture and will identify themselves with ministries that they watch on television and have no personal interaction with.

Are you ready for another funny story? I was in a store and struck up a conversation with a woman. At some point the conversation turned to places of worship. Most pastors can attest to the fact that when people find out you are a pastor, they sometimes start making excuses for why they don't go to church. As we were talking, I asked what church she attended because she looked very familiar. She started down the rabbit trail of church hurt stories but what came out next was comical yet very common.

She said her pastor was the great visionary Bishop T.D Jakes. Now mind you, we live in the state of Ohio so I doubt very highly that she would be afforded the frequent opportunity to hear his familiar refrain, *"Get ready, get ready, get ready!"* in person. She was a textbook example of the seeker who has a connection in the heart but for whom one-on-one interaction is unnecessary. The seeker friendly attitude is "just feed me and when I choose not to eat, I will not turn you on." Television and social media are great in this context for giving seeker friendly Believers the opportunity to feast from the tables of great men and women of God. The problem is that it can enable the seeker friendly person to stay in the mode of seeking without committing to a local body.

If commitment is not your desire at

> *She said her pastor was the great visionary Bishop T.D Jakes. Now mind you, we live in the state of Ohio so I doubt very highly that she would be afforded the frequent opportunity to hear his infamous stanza, "Get ready, get ready, get ready!" in person. She was a textbook example of the seeker who has a connection in the heart but for whom one-on-one interaction is unnecessary.*

the present moment, then the seeker-friendly culture will likely appeal to you. But allow me to caution and remind you of Hebrews 10:25 NKJV: *"Not forsaking the assembling of ourselves together, as the manner of some is; but exhorting one another: and so much the more, as ye see the day is approaching."* Seek and you will find; connect and you will grow.

9. **Prophetic Culture** is closely related to the charismatic culture in the sense that you might notice many facets of the five-fold ministry gifts in operation. When you are pastor of a prophetic culture, it does not mean that prophetic words will be released at every worship service. As a pastor of a prophetic culture, I can attest to the fact that sometimes the Holy Spirit will interrupt a service with a revelatory Word that may drop in my spirit.

In a prophetic culture, the move of the Holy Spirit is of utmost importance. In order for the prophetic culture to function properly, it is necessary for the Holy Spirit to flow. Prophecy is the revealed Word of God, therefore, when a spiritual house is formed around the company of prophetic revelations, one must be comfortable if the Holy Spirit changes direction midstream. The traditional will not be comfortable in this type of atmosphere, considering how the flow is governed by timing. In addition to that, the necessary revelations needed for the house, are not just for members of that particular house but for anyone who graced the premises on that particular day. I cannot tell you how many times the Spirit has invaded the atmosphere during business meetings, Bible studies, and any time the saints have come together.

Prophetic cultures encourage the use of your senses in hearing from God. The atmosphere in this culture is set through worship and intercession. Prophetic cultures survive off intentional time in prayer petitioning the Holy Spirit to reveal His will. Prophetic cultures will equip those who want to hear from God and who want to become equipped to release through different means.

> *In order for the prophetic culture to function properly, it is necessary for the Holy Spirit to flow. Prophecy is the revealed Word of God, therefore, when a spiritual house is formed around the company of prophetic revelations, one must be comfortable if the Holy Spirit changes direction midstream.*

Joel 2:28 NKJV reads "And it shall come to pass in the last days, says God, that I will pour out of My Spirit on all flesh: and your sons and your daughters will prophesy, and your young men shall see visions, and your old men shall dream dreams."

If you are connected to the atmosphere of the prophetic culture and have the desire to hear from God in different, multiple ways, the anointing here will open your Spirit and you will receive. This does not mean you will acquire the prophetic gifting but if you are truly unified with the prophetic culture, you will have other spiritual senses opened.

CHAPTER 5

———◆◆◆———

THE LORD IS MY SHEPHERD: THE WAY OF THE SHEEP

In sermon after sermon we have been inclined to hear the description of sheep as weak, innocent animals. Sheep were a valuable commodity in Israel. I believe many times people have a hard time relating to sheep because it requires the average person to envision through an agricultural mindset, which is far removed from most modern-day Believers. I must admit my concept of animals is usually connected to the zoo! So to get me to conceptualize my life as an animal - especially an animal that seems weak by the world's standard - takes effort. Even pondering the fact that sheep are so valuable to God at times seemed implausible until I matured in Christ. As I've grown in the Word and in life, I've also come to realize that the nature of sheep is not that of ignorance nor weakness, but of vulnerability, dependency, and humility all of which expose dependency.

On a flight coming home from a speaking engagement in Alabama, I had the pleasure of being seated next to a kind young man who just happened to be a farmer. I hope that there are some preachers reading this because you can appreciate how the inner witness leapt inside me when I asked him about his vocation. Having grown up in Ohio, I never went to the Ohio State Fair, which is a serious event each year, so you can probably guess what my first question was.

"What type of farmer are you?"

"A grain farmer."

"Why grain over dairy or meat farmer?"

His response to dairy was that it was of no interest to him. He then gave the answer as to why he wasn't a meat farmer. Then I said from somewhere, "Tell me about sheep."

> *As I've grown in the Word and in life, I've also come to realize that the nature of sheep is not that of ignorance nor weakness, but of vulnerability, dependency, and humility all of which expose dependency.*

He said, "There is a running joke between farmers on why you never want to be a sheep farmer. Sheep are born to die." When I asked what he meant, he replied, "When sheep get sick, they don't look to find healing, they isolate themselves and go off and die." Afterward, he chuckled and said, "They would rather die than try to get better." I thought *young man you don't know what you are saying*! I was hearing from God right in the middle of the air.

In my Spirit, I envisioned believers doing exactly the same thing. If they are not careful, during the times when they find themselves in a state of confusion, weariness or doubt, isolation will be more appealing than revelation. True revelation comes from the Word of God and the Word says we are all like sheep that have gone astray, and, in our wandering, we may experience the feeling of sickness away from the Great Shepherd. This two- and-a-half-hour flight brought a new revelation of how we, in this modern age, have not grasped the love of God in the sense that He laid down His life for us (His sheep). Jesus became the sacrificial Lamb of God so we wouldn't have to go off and die on our own. His sacrifice was given for us while we were yet in our sinful state.

As my flight companion and I continued in our dialogue about sheep, he stated multiple times that it takes a certain type of farmer to raise sheep. It requires a nurturing nature which is beneficial to the caring and the overall needs of the sheep. Again, in my Spirit I heard the Lord. He knows our needs as sheep, and that is why He has stated "I will not fail you nor forsake you" (Joshua 1:5). He kept His promise through allowing Jesus to walk with the disciples. After His earthy assignment was fulfilled, He continued to fulfill His promise by sending the Gift of the Holy Spirit.

> *This two- and-a-half-hour flight brought a new revelation of how we, in this modern age, have not grasped the love of God in the sense that He laid down His life for us (His sheep). Jesus became the sacrificial Lamb of God so we wouldn't have to go off and die on our own.*

What man has not truly comprehended is the strength of sheep! It is apparent that in the mind of many believers are the orchestrated images of sheep struggling instead of being triumphant. Yet Scripture states *"But if the Spirit of Him that raised up Jesus from the dead dwell in you, He that raised up Christ from the dead shall also quicken your mortal bodies by His Spirit that dwelleth in you"* (Romans 8:11). As sheep, we have an untapped power source residing in us. This source is so powerful that the grave could not contain it. That means every spiritual force sent to stop the resurrection was defeated. Now picture that power inside of you!

CHAPTER 6

———◆———

YEA THOU I WALK: INTERRUPTED COFFEE BREAK

While taking what I believe all pastors need - some *"me time"* - I packed my bags, told the family so long for a few days, boarded a plane, and headed to a three-day prophetic conference in Tulsa. Rest, renewal, and re-igniting the fire inside were my goals for this trip. Rising early and turning in late was perfectly fine with me! Scheduled lectures began promptly at 9:00 am. The lecture hall filled up fast that to get a good seat you had to come early. Even though every presenter was engaging, after sitting for more than two hours before our first scheduled break, it was obvious that I and dozens of other attendees needed to stretch our legs or get a morning jolt of coffee.

On the second day of the conference during the scheduled break, I took the escalator to the Starbucks in the hotel's lobby only to find that nearly 40-50 others had the same idea. The line was extremely long, but I let patience have her perfect work. The smells of coffee brewing and my mouth watering for a caramel macchiato kept my feet planted in line. I was not prepared for what came next.

> *I said, "My mother has always said if you have nothing good to say, then say nothing." I looked past her shoulder to see if the line had moved. Everything inside me wanted to scream "Hurry up behind the counter so I can escape!"*

While waiting patiently for the lone Starbucks worker, I should have petitioned God to help her "do all things." Finally help came to assist the employee. But in the meantime, I was approached by a warm but overly friendly woman who greeted me by asking, "Are you enjoying the conference?" I quickly responded that I was so glad I had a chance to attend and even though it was only my second day, I wanted to come the following year. This tall robust woman smiled in response to my statement. Seemingly out of nowhere, she began to express with boldness and confidence her admiration for a public figure who I believe exhibits a lack of integrity, a spirit of divisiveness, and amoral character that are all in direct **OPPOSITION** to that of a Christian. I didn't respond as she went on to say, "He doesn't take anything from anybody, and he means what he says." Again, no response from me - please can I just get some coffee?

She pressed on "You're not saying anything, and what is *that look* for?"

I thought, *"Am I getting pranked? I must be on camera!"*

The inquisitive look on her face demanded a response.

I said, "My mother has always said if you have nothing good to say, then say nothing." I looked past her shoulder to see if the line had moved. Everything inside me wanted to scream *"Hurry up behind the counter so I can escape!"* I wanted this conversation to end. Even though this was a prophetic conference she must not have heard from the Holy Spirit because she was insistent on my responding to her statements. If she had heard from the Holy Spirit, He would have told her to stop. Now before you throw this book down, I am only going to talk about her approaching me about the character of a man.

Finally I said, "Well ma'am, I am blessed to be married to a Godly man, and God has blessed us to be the proud parents of two young men which are less than two years apart in age. They have their own rooms, their own electronic devices and their own friends and their own favorite foods in the refrigerator. When I go to the grocery store, I ask if there is anything special anyone would like me to bring home. When I return, it is understood if one son wants what the other has chosen, he is to ask his brother if he will share. It has been instilled that you don't take anything without asking . . . If I am teaching my sons to honor their own brother's space, I have a hard time sharing your sentiment. I don't think it is acceptable to make glib sexist statements about women and constantly post and use divisive rhetoric . . .

> *Before she could get a word in, I continued,*
> *"The Bible teaches us that if we are at fault, we are to confess our*
> *sins one to another. Ma'am, I don't hate the man, as a matter*
> *of fact I pray for the man, but his character is unquestionably*
> *contrary to biblical principles and integrity. 2 Timothy 1:7 says*
> *'God gave us not a spirit of fear but of power*
> *and of love and self-control.'*
> *I was trying to let my silence speak for itself."*

But now that I felt backed into a corner with her intrusive insistence, I was feeling bolder in the Spirit with each word. "And what do you mean he doesn't back down from his words, you never said anything about godliness or his ability to be a role model for all men? From what I have seen, he has not exhibited the character that I would call role model material for my sons. Godly character produces patience, temperance self- control and many other fruits of the spirit." I petitioned her for some of her time since she was allotted some of mine. I asked if she had heard his reference to a former co-host on a major television networks as a big fat pig. Immediately after I asked the question it was *her* face that needed fixing!

It seemed as if the woman believed her barrage of questions to me was acceptable and *required* answers, but her silence was deafening when faced with mine. It was not my intention to be confrontational, but I wanted an explanation for her unsolicited opinions. Of course she had none, and after a few more comparisons that showed the weakness of her rhetoric, I was finally at the front of the line. But what does this interrupted coffee break have to do with ministry cultures, sheep, shepherds, or anything else we're discussing? Let me see if I can make the connection.

This woman had learned from a culture – perhaps in her home, her church, her friendship circle, her work environment – that it was acceptable to spout her opinions and to expect others to respond. She had met me in a line waiting for coffee but immediately felt entitled enough to drag me into a conversation that would require me to share my personal, political, religious, or other opinions. *And she didn't even know me!* But when the tables were turned on her and I didn't keep silent nor agree with her, the cultural habit she thought would sustain her proved weak and left her in the vulnerable position to which she had tried to relegate me. One culture or several had taught her that this type of behavior was okay.

This same type of interaction can happen when there are cultural clashes in types of worship. For example when those who are comfortable in a traditional culture might try to force their ideals into a contemporary culture and expect them to be accepted without question or resistance. Or the expectation might be that the contemporary culture will explain or defend their way of worship. The truth is that no culture has to explain, defend, or clarify *why* they exist. That's a part of the freedom that Christ provided when He died on Calvary and rose with all power. While we might never agree on which culture style of worship is "best" or most conducive, we can also never think or act as if OURS is above any other.

CHAPTER 7

---◆◆◆---

HE PREPARES A TABLE: WHY WE EAT WHAT WE DO

In previous chapters we have discussed cultures in places of worship. Now we will dissect what attracts Believers to certain cultures or places of worship. Is it that we see something of ourselves or something that we need? Do we identify with others who attend? Or is it simply a matter of *personality* or *character*? This is what I want to consider here: the choices we make based on personality and character. Both of these choices are absolutely personal, but I want to give you the tools to at least identify the impetus for YOUR decisions in this arena.

Personality is what makes you a unique person and is recognizable soon after your birth. Psychologist believe that there are several personality types, two of the most readily identifiable being the introvert and the extrovert. Both types have layers attached to them which can dictate how the person reacts, processes, and perpetrates events in life. Character, on the other hand, is what is formed through life's circumstances, environments, and belief systems. I usually describe character as an inner traffic light. Red which means stop, do not proceed. Yellow meaning you should proceed with caution when (something) doesn't sit well in your spirit. Green tells you it's okay to proceed - all restraints are removed.

If I were to ask you to look back at some of your personal connections in life, those that were chosen by you, were they chosen based off your personality preference or character preference? If your choices are based on personality it may be centered on your comfort level, senses, and appetites. This choice is not wrong but instead reveals the comfort with and dependence on familiarity. Being a big fan of animal documentaries, I cannot count how many Saturdays I've watched shows about different species of animals. Different species that are raised together from birth inevitably have the ability to cohabitate, but ultimately the time to be acclimated back into their natural environment arrives. Nature kicks in and they adapt to God's designed habitation and usually readily adapt to a more natural familial group. The influence of adaptation is powerful.

I am an introvert by nature so for me to co-pastor with my

> *Personality is what makes you a unique person and is recognizable soon after your birth. Character is what is formed through life's circumstances, environments, and belief systems. I usually describe character as an inner traffic light. Red which means stop, do not proceed. Yellow meaning you should proceed with caution when (something) doesn't sit well in your spirit. Green tells you it's okay to proceed - all restraints are removed.*

husband for over nine years at the time of this writing seems to contradict my personality. But it is absolutely in line with my character. God can use introverts to proclaim His word without having to change their personality to fit the call. Even though I am an introvert, I come alive when ministering the Gospel. As soon as ministry is over, I go back into my shell.

I held a prophetic retreat a few years ago at which time we took personality assessments. I discovered that I was the textbook case of an introvert. I am not the one to run and sit in the front seat. As a matter of fact, it took me years to call myself a prophet, and it wasn't because I didn't believe God birthed me with the gift. I was just uncomfortable attaching a label to my call. It wasn't until the words God spoke through my lips came to pass and others began to refer to me by the call on my life that I felt comfortable declaring it.

As a pastor, there are times when I must push past my natural tendency to be a little aloof – which is also a characteristic of introverts. I do align with the Proverb that if you want a friend you must show yourself friendly. I used to fleece God by petitioning if He *really* called me to pastor because it was never my desire, nor did it fit my personality Here's a nugget: every call requires us to be on the potter's wheel. When the potter starts to mold you for His divine purpose, it will usually feel uncomfortable. If comfort is the only catalyst for saying "yes" to the call, then the struggle in answering the call will be intensified. I don't know of any whose names are written in the Biblical Hall of Fame where excitement was part of their call to fame.

If your choices are character-based, then you can surmise it is centered around inward values. Values are a set of standards that may never have to be proclaimed but are easily observed through one's actions and decisions. Character is what many describe as actions that are done in private. E. M. Bounds describes character as "the inner life of a person which forms actions and shapes lives." God gives us private times alone with Him to develop our character into His divine will for our lives.

Here's a nugget: every call requires us to be on the potter's wheel. When the potter starts to mold you for His divine purpose, it will usually feel uncomfortable.

If we allow private correction, we will obtain public promotion. As Believers mature in their spiritual walk, they grow in the understanding that worship is connected to divine correction. God chastens those whom He loves. Being the perfect role model of fatherhood, He in no way wants our character flaws to be exposed. So, he disciplines in private.

Can you imagine our parents' reaction if while they were disciplining us, we started to thank them because we know that it is for our good? Imagine how it would make their heart sink to know that you understand. They must discipline you because they love you. Abba Father wants that type of response from us because in the long run it will strengthen and equip us for His divine will in our lives. Private correction is godly character building, produces humility and humility always precedes promotion. The awesomeness of God is so overwhelming that He will speak and correct in the secret place. His mercy extends to such a level that He allows you to find the secret place and He will meet you there.

The first step in developing Godly character is desiring intimacy with God. This is the place where your worship becomes such a valuable source of strength that when it is not present there is a sense of emptiness. Whenever one talks about being empty it is always viewed as a negative, but in the spirit realm it may indicate a deficiency of intimacy with the Father. As a person with chronic anemia I can always tell when my blood is at a very low level. I become very sluggish, my body temperature changes, and my craving for certain foods start to reoccur. I will crave ice, flour and anything salty because my body is releasing signals that it's time for a recharge.

This craving or feeling of emptiness or deprivation usually does not happen overnight. The buildup has been coming. When you are spiritually empty, you will hunger for the four-course meal. Sweets alone will not suffice. The (re)filling is achieved when worship evolves into service, but not in a simple way. This type of service is what the prophet Isaiah so eloquently described in Isaiah 40:31a *"they that wait on the Lord shall renew their strength."*

Waiting in this sense is like taking on the role of a waiter, standing patiently for God to give His desired order, or to reveal his perfect will. A trained waiter doesn't attempt to change the order but

> *If we allow private correction, we will obtain public promotion. As Believers mature in their spiritual walk, they grow in the understanding that worship is connected to divine correction. God chastens those whom He loves. Being the perfect role model of fatherhood, He in no way wants our character flaws to be exposed. So, he disciplines in private.*

repeats the order for clarity and once prepared, delivers it and once again repeats for clarity. When we wait on God, we can bring back to His remembrance what He ordered, or told us to do, and be strengthened or renewed each time we do. We must continue to come to God in anticipation to see if He is pleased with our service or if there is anything else that we can bring Him.

We must not demand a tip (blessing) but instead believe that if our service warrants it, we will receive in the name of Jesus. If we approach the Lord in this posture, there is no way possible that a blessing will not be waiting on the table for us. Isaiah, the prophet, is a Biblical mentor of mine. He was asked by God, "Who would go for us? Who shall we send?" My hero responded, "Here am I! Send me!" Before he was launched into what God called him to do, Isaiah's character was symbolically purged, cleansed, and corrected through the laying of red, hot coals on his tongue (Isaiah 6:1-8). The purification of his lips was the part of the ordination of his voice which was needed for his kingdom assignment.

As I began this chapter, I began by stating that we are free will agents. As free will agents who can make choices, we have been afforded the freedom to choose who we follow spiritually, whether the connection is based on personality or character. It is still a personal choice. The freedom comes from acknowledging our reason and being able to live with it.

CHAPTER 8

———◆·◆———

THY ROD & THY STAFF: THE SHEEP OF HIS PASTURE

As we have considered various cultures and what can influence our choices when it comes to choosing a place to call our ministry home, I want to now offer for your consideration that there are also various types of sheep. In this chapter, I have categorized sheep (members of church/ministry families) into five groups:

1. New Convert Sheep
2. Wayward Sheep
3. Needy Sheep
4. Rebellious Sheep
5. Dedicated Sheep

Understand that my descriptions are not absolute but have been created based on years of observation from the eyes of a church member and a pastor.

1. *New Convert Sheep* represent brothers and sisters who have experienced an awakening from our Lord and Savior Jesus Christ. This happens after they have made peace with God. Scripture states in *2 Corinthians 5:18 NASB "Now all these things are from God, whom reconciled us to Himself through Christ and gave us the ministry of reconciliation."* There are two types of peace that Believers obtain. The first type of peace mentioned is making peace *with* God. Until we make the free will decision to accept Jesus Christ as our Lord and Savior, we still reside in a broken state. Peace with God releases the righteousness of God which qualifies us to become Kingdom beneficiaries. God's desire is for His Kingdom to come and His will to be done in the earth as it is in Heaven. When we choose to make peace with God, we start the process of releasing the Kingdom of God on earth. His will shall be established by His children.

   When the believer receives the peace of God as described in *Romans 5:1 NASB "Therefore, having been justified by faith, we have peace with God through our Lord Jesus Christ,"* we walk in the second type of peace – the peace of justification (just as if they had never sinned). Our faith is what qualifies us to receive pardon for our sins and separation from sin. Unlike having *made peace with God,* which requires a confession and turning away (repentance), the peace of justification requires the Believer to walk by faith and along the journey peace will be released. I believe conversion experiences are all personal and no one's experience should be dismissed or undervalued.

When shepherding the *New Convert,* you may notice many things take place in their lives which will be revealed in their actions. I have witnessed excitement over the awakening experience that is taking place in their lives. I have likened it to watching an 8-month-old baby on Facebook receive hearing aids and experiencing what most of us take for granted for the first time. It literally brought me to tears watching this mother holding her son in her arms as the doctor placed the first hearing aid in. The baby squirmed and cried at the invasion taking place against him. Yet the doctor never stopped the procedure. I watched the mother place a pacifier in her son's mouth to try to alleviate any discomfort he may be experiencing. But she did not try to stop the procedure because she knew it would make her child's life better.

> *Until we make the free will decision to accept Jesus Christ as our Lord and Savior, we still reside in a broken state. Peace with God releases the righteousness of God which qualifies us to become Kingdom beneficiaries.*

After the first hearing aid was placed in, the doctor spoke. The baby's eyes got as big as saucers because he heard something for the first time. The more the doctor spoke the baby began to cry. This is what made me cry. When the mother began to speak, the baby started to smile. His eyes grew even wider as he watched his mother's mouth move. Others in the room started to release comforting words to the baby and his innate senses kicked in. He began to look around for the location of the new noise. He cried at other's voices. But every time his mother's voice started again, he would look directly at her mouth and the most beautiful wide smile would reappear.

I believe this is how the *New Convert* responds to the voices that swirl around all of us each and every day. The vast majority of them probably seem uncomfortable, not trustworthy, or dangerous, but when the Father speaks you witness a change of their whole countenance. I love to see their excitement from revelation and the love of the Father on a *New Convert*. I have also observed how God builds their faith by answering their prayers and preforming miracles for them.

Eager to help in the church, *New Converts* usually make statements like: "Pastor whatever you want me to do I will do." I always tell them, "Slow down, God is not going anywhere." Many times shepherds ignore the Scripture's warning that those who are tasked with responsibilities in ministry *"must not be a recent convert, or he may become conceited and fall under the same judgment as the devil"* (I Timothy 3:6 NIV). This scripture was spoken to young Timothy who was given a church that was already in existence. It was not a small church either!

The Apostle Paul was instructing Timothy not to place a new convert into a leadership position until they have matured. It required the testing of their faith, lest they become prey to the enemy's devices. The devil has no new tricks just different devices to catch his intended victims. The original device was pride and it is still the number one device today. Shepherds must be careful that the exuberance of the *New Convert* doesn't cause them to burn out too fast. Let them grow as you show them how to be faithful in God's work and lead them to examples in the Word as well as in the local body where they can be mentored. It is important to cover them in this stage.

New Converts are extremely impressionable and vulnerable. They will look to others for advice, guidance and mentoring. But shepherds have a chief responsibility to be extremely watchful over these new sheep. Jesus warned in a parable that the best intentions are often compromised by the enemy's interference. **"But while everyone**

> *I believe this is how the New Convert responds to the voices that swirl around all of us each and every day. The vast majority of them probably seem uncomfortable, not trustworthy, or dangerous, but when the Father speaks you witness a change of their whole countenance.*

was sleeping, his enemy came and sowed weeds among the wheat, and went away" (Matthew 13:25 NIV). In defense of many well-meaning shepherds whose mission is to sow the Word so that the body of Christ may grow, they often overlook tares that carry titles and hold positions without the Anointing that should accompany those titles and positions. I'm not only speaking about leaders with titles: I am talking about Believers who carry the title of Christian!

That title carries more weight than all the rest. The other titles are our assignments on earth, but the title of Christian carries the responsibility of developing the characteristics of the Father as spelled out in the Word of God and manifested in the life and earthly ministry of Jesus Christ. When questioned by the accusatory Pharisees as to when the Kingdom of God would come Jesus replied, *"The coming of the kingdom of God is not something that can be observed, nor will people say, "Here it is, or "There it is because the kingdom of God is in your midst"* (Luke 17:20-21 NIV). We should not instill a spirit of suspicion in the *New Convert*. Instead we should instill a dependency on the Holy Spirit to protect them from the tares sent to steal nourishment from them and to ultimately choke out their new-found excitement in their relationship with Christ.

2. *Wayward Sheep* are unpredictable. This type of sheep is basically those who have been in the family of Believers

for years (but New Converts can fall into this category too). The shepherd must be very careful in dealing with the Wayward Sheep who has been saved for a while and the one who has just come to salvation. When they are seasoned (as opposed to mature) and life has seasoned them, it is sometimes life captures their attention more than the things of the Spirit. The *Wayward* struggle with having impulsive natures. The *Wayward* are textbook examples of the prodigal son who was captivated – and soon captured - by the cares of this world. The world captures believers through setbacks, financial worries, life issues, assigned attacks, and anything that produces separation.

When exegeting the story of the prodigal son, we do not read that his family had done him wrong or that there was a legitimate reason for his departure. His decision was in part based upon his attraction of the unknown. The Lord has given all His children an imagination but until it is sanctified, our natural-born-into-sin-nature will war against our God-given creative-nature. The prodigal son did not take captive the enticing luring effects of the world. Instead, he asked to be released into it and his desire was granted.

> *Wayward sheep are very unpredictable. They struggle with impulsive natures.*

When dealing with this type of sheep, you may be given the privilege of being told why they are leaving but their normal action will be to just silently walk away. Many *Wayward* sheep may not be able to articulate why they aren't coming to church regularly. It is difficult to explain "I've been enticed; not mad, just curious to see if I am missing something." The *Wayward* can be enticed by vocations, by the captivating preacher that comes in town, or a new relationship.

Just like the prodigal son who came to himself when all was lost, the *Wayward Sheep* might show up again at your church. When dealing with this group of individuals, the shepherd cannot take their wayward behaviors personally. Their waywardness is due to the fact they have not placed their soul under subjection. Putting ones' soul under subjection requires the confession of an unsettled nature. This confession starts with God and will lead to repentance. When true repentance takes place, the *Wayward* will possess the ability to resist the temptation of feeling guilty for their actions. This happens because their actions are not intentionally directed toward wounding their leaders. They understand and accept that they are just spiritually immature and become willing to be still long enough to grow up.

3. *Needy Sheep*, at first glance, might get labeled as the previously mentioned group. This is merely due to the many similarities between the two. The major similarity is that they find nothing wrong with treating the church like a revolving door society where their needs/wants are supposed to be met at all costs. What they really

should say is *"Pastor, you need to read my mind!"* This group might not leave the ministry permanently because they really like where they are, they're just needy. They usually like to be acknowledged for what they contribute to the ministry. By that I mean, their names must be called if they are on a committee. The *Needy* sometimes frustrate themselves as a result of self-imposed high expectations.

This group can also be territorial. I once had someone say to me, **"Pastor I don't want our church to grow because I like having you all to myself."** I thought oh no, I must stop you in your tracks and cancel that word curse. I responded, "Sister, if we don't grow then we will die." I do believe that things can be at a standstill sometimes but in no way should someone desire to

> *His decision was in part based upon his attraction of the unknown. The Lord has given all His children an imagination but until it is sanctified, our natural-born-into-sin-nature will war against our God-given creative-nature.*

stay in dying place. I said, "I choose not to live in Lodebar" (reference from 2 Samuel 9). Her thought may have been perfectly harmless to her, but her need to be seen and touched, not by the spirit but by handshakes and hugs, was the root of her value system.

Being *Needy* is a state of mind essentially because something is missing which causes the *Needy* to crave interaction. When I first began in ministry, I led youth groups and taught Sunday school. I was in my early twenties, single, and had time at my disposal so that I could devote a lot of energy to the young ladies. Due to our constant interaction, I became very close with them. When God called my husband and I to minister together, a few of the young ladies joined us which wasn't the problem.

The struggle came when they insisted on trying to hold me hostage to our previous roles and relationship. I was bombarded with the pains of my struggle to be released from the old. What I desired was to enter the new without wounding or giving in to their demands of what had become comfortable to them. The discomfort with *Needy Sheep* stems from the inability to accept the evolutionary nature of all relationships. The process of formation or growth, or evolution, can be offensive to Believers when it comes to our church/ministry relationships.

> *The major similarity is that they find nothing wrong with treating the church like a revolving door society where their needs/wants are supposed to be met at all costs. What they really should say is "Pastor, you need to read my mind!" This group might not leave the ministry permanently and the truth is they really like where they are, they're just needy.*

Maturing in Christ calls for us to evolve through a growth process. This is achieved when the Needy strive to walk in the footsteps of Jesus and His proclamation, *"I did not come to be served but to serve,"* even though He could have required people to serve Him. Scripture instructs us to *"humble ourselves under the mighty hand of God and in due season He will exalt us if we faint not"* (I Peter 5:6 NKJV). Jesus' due season was performing miracles, being a great prophet, teacher and apostle who ultimately defeated death, hell and the grave. He modeled what Believers should strive to become: people of humility and authority.

The exact opposite is being needy - always expecting your needs to be met at others expense. I remember my spiritual father in the Lord saying, "You have to learn to shear the sheep and milk the goats." In other words, use your energy wisely. I have found one culprit for pastoral burnout is desiring more for the sheep than they desire for themselves. I do believe that a change can and will come, but only through submission to the Holy Spirit. When ministering to the *Needy*, patience and long suffering are two Fruit of the Spirit necessary for having a harmonious relationship.

4. *Rebellious Sheep* operate in a spirit of control which can render them unteachable unless they are delivered. At times they may display haughty spirits that are fueled by dissension. What is so amazing about this group is the fact that sometimes they don't realize the level of control they are under! When *Rebellious Sheep* are present in church cultures, they will sometimes entangle others by enticing them to look through their very selfish, petty,

fractured lens. Rebellion breeds rebellion, and it will not stop with one operative. It will enlist other agents to do its dirty work. It usually starts out very subtly with clever deception. They will exhibit strong body language and disrupt the flow of service by their late arrival. When the *Rebellious Sheep* becomes agitated, they will not be able to look you in the face or have open dialogue simply because their spirit is agitated. Unlike the *Wayward* which blow in and out like a breeze flowing over our Great Lakes, the *Rebellious* stay and try to make others either conform with them, rebel, or become uncomfortable.

I have been enlightened by stories told from those who have witnessed this type of diabolical spirit. The *Rebellious* withhold tithes and offerings from their place of worship thinking it will change the culture of the church, not realizing they are cursing themselves with a curse (Malachi 3:9). The enemy is so crafty

> *Rebellious Sheep operate in a spirit of control which can render them unteachable unless they are delivered. At times they may display haughty spirits that are fueled by dissension. What is so amazing about this group is the fact that sometimes they don't realize the level of control they are under.*

in his strategies that he will cause the *Rebellious* to harm themselves in their attempt to gain control. Holding back what belongs to God is not only foolish, it is has long term detrimental effects.

A rebellious spirit is easily observed. It will seldom admit being wrong, is hypercritical, and finds fault in every situation or person who disagrees with it or shines a light of truth on its motives. Unless it is called out and canceled, it will continue. An effective strategy in dealing with the *Rebellious Sheep* is to pray for keen discernment, courage, and temperance. This serves as an aid in equipping leaders to harness this spirit by the righteousness of God, through authority, and tough love.

5. ***Dedicated Sheep*** are devoted to a task or purpose, having single-minded loyalty or integrity. Their service is always motivated by the Scripture that reads ***"with good will doing service, as to the Lord, and not to men"*** (Ephesians 6:7 NKJV). Unpacking the style of the *Dedicated* could take hours because they are the most overlooked, overworked, under-appreciated group in our local assemblies. Yet they are the most stable – and invaluable - of all the groups.

It has been my observation that this group is the foundation of any church. In the process of building a house, most homeowners are concerned with the foundation in the initial building stage. Although I have not had the privilege of building a home yet, whenever I see poured foundations while driving by new construction sites, I know the next phase is the dwelling portion of the house. That means the aesthetics are on the way and the vision is now taking shape.

The foundation may not be pretty in that it shows only the base of the home. But it must surely be level, must match the designed blueprints, and must meet building codes. Foundations can only be poured when the weather is conducive. Spiritually speaking, that explains why so many believers are exhausted, frustrated and anxious. Either they have attempted to build with the wrong materials or out of alignment with the current season. Understanding the timing of sowing and reaping is crucial when building from ground up.

In the same vein, when building upon existing foundations it is vitally important to have them examined. This will reveal any cracks, damages or structural issues that have may gone unnoticed or unattended. If the foundation is not examined, eventually these cracks, damages and structural issues will alter the intended design and purpose of the foundation. Its designed purpose is to hold up the vision of the structure. It is likewise in the body of Christ. Over time, in the natural, as foundations begin to settle, the cracks and other structural issues may arise. For that very reason a contractor will tell you before any major renovation process begins, the foundation must be checked to see if it is stable enough to handle the changes. I believe that many truths that apply to the natural also apply in the spirit.

> *Unpacking the style of the Dedicated could take hours because they are the most overlooked, overworked, under-appreciated group in our local assemblies. Yet they are the most stable – and invaluable - of all the groups.*

Foundations in the spirit need to be maintained through prayer and genuine concern for maintaining the mission of the ministry. *Dedicated Sheep* need to have the vision set before them periodically to remind them of the contributions they have made as well as future plans because this group can become creatures of habit. I liken it to gardening (which is not one of my gifts). You will never hear me brag about having a green thumb and in light of this, I only plant perennials. I must admit gardening is relaxing yet I truly know my limitations.

After living in my house for over sixteen years, last summer I ventured out and did a little gardening. I researched the different types of flowers to make sure they would survive the vision I had for my yard. I cannot recall the countless instructions I read to make sure I would pick the right one. I then ventured out to our local home goods store, walk straight to the gardening department without hesitation and found myself attracted to vast array of colors. It was inevitable that frustration would set in and I would come home empty handed. I was determined to have flowers and durability won out over beauty.

My pursuit of purchasing flowers made me appreciate the importance of location – i.e., finding your place and getting planted. As the time came for me to embark upon my backyard adventure, I looked for the perfect spot, dug holes, removed the flowers from their previous containers, loosed the dirt, and prepared the roots for their next dwelling place. After placing them in the desired spot, I added all of the necessary nourishments to help them survive in their assigned surroundings. I even supplied additional soil containing additives that the topsoil might be lacking.

Upon completion, I supplied a generous amount of water to hydrate and help aid the flowers in surviving in its new surroundings. Maintenance, with my choice of perennials, would include periodically removing any hindrances (weeds) that could interfere with the flowers' growth. At the end of the season, I would remove all debris and expect to see their return the next season.

My choice for perennials is not only because they come back year after year, but low maintenance is required for these type flowers to survive. Sometimes *Dedicated Sheep* get treated like perennials and are expected to be on their assignment, stay planted in their assignment, while also weathering any storms

> *The foundation may not be pretty in that it shows only the base of the home. But it must surely be level, must match the designed blueprints, and must meet building codes. Foundations can only be poured when the weather is conducive. Spiritually speaking, that explains why so many believers are exhausted, frustrated and anxious. Either they have attempted to build with the wrong materials or out of alignment with the current season. Understanding the timing of sowing and reaping is crucial when building from ground up.*

that may come. And of course, they are expected to ALWAYS be present!

In the formation process of our ministry we began with four dedicated women, my husband and me. The four dedicated women are still with us to this day. They serve as the ministry secretary, treasurer, administrator, and doorkeeper. All of these positions are undervalued by the average church goer. Secretaries are responsible for all correspondence that pertain to the ministry. They are the mail carriers, the compiler of the bulletins, and often the liaison between the church and the pastor. If you want to find out their level of authority, make a church secretary mad and your event may never make it off their desk!

The treasurer's responsibilities include but are not limited to maintaining the financial records of the church by keeping receipts, payroll, and paying monthly expenses of the ministry. I purposely omitted the one duty performed every time there is an offering – the "finance department huddle" where they huddle together in their assigned guarded room and count all money, making sure each and every penny is accounted for. While everyone is mingling after church deciding what's for dinner those in the finance department are counting. Sometimes the counting takes place during service times. They deposit all funds and are responsible for preparing and providing the crucial end-of-the-year financial statements which contain all collected donations for each individual.

The administrator holds the daunting duty maintaining the organizational structure of ministries. They must be objective in how they approach needs, issues, clashes, disagreements, or visions of in-house ministries/auxiliaries. The administrator works closely with leadership and the pastoral staff of any church. I consider them to be spiritual silent partners with the pastor.

The final group to be discussed are the doorkeepers which are often referred to as ushers. They are the first people that you encounter when you attend any church **Psalm 84:10 NASB "For a day in Your courts is better than a thousand outside. I would rather stand at the threshold of**

> *Sometimes Dedicated Sheep get treated like perennials and are expected to be on their assignment, stay planted in their assignment, while also weathering any storms that may come. And of course, they are expected to ALWAYS be present!*

the house of my God than dwell in the tents of the wickedness." They are the first to arrive and usually last to leave due to the fact that they must attend to any ministry members or visitors' lacking in home training. You will find the doorkeepers picking up articles that seem to be lost and benches, chairs or the floor become their final resting place. The doorkeepers should in their calling possess the ability to display the heart of the pastor through their welcome and reception of all who grace the church.

Dedicated Sheep are the pillars of the church and the solid rocks on which the natural church stands. Let's call them the "Peters" of the church (reference to Jesus' strong disciple). They see and hear more than we can imagine yet they are never *wayward, rebellious and needy.* They have matured beyond being the *new convert.* Purposing in my heart to get feedback from this group has caused me to work smarter and not harder. Possessing a discipleship mentality, *Dedicated Sheep* will be honest when posed with questions about me, as Pastor, or the ministry.

Even though they may be the foundation, the perennials (the pillars and silent agents), *Dedicated Sheep* still have needs. Their strength, consistency, and dependability do not make them void of the need for attention and love that is so lavished on the others who often demand it. If you are part of the *Dedicated Sheep*, schedule an appointment every now with the pastor. If that is not possible due to the size of the ministry, schedule one with a leader who has can pass on Godly information with wisdom and discernment. The appointment doesn't have to be about concerns but can be about life and about keeping the foundation intact. We all get cracks that will turn into holes if not attended to.

In ministering to *Dedicated Sheep* where relationships go beyond church membership to the family, keep in mind family gets overlooked more than any other group, and this group becomes extended family. Over a period of time I have realized that I need to have office hours.

The majority of the appointments are with the four other groups because often, *Dedicated Sheep* don't want to bother leadership and they feel like they have been equipped enough to make it through. I've repeatedly heard the statement from this group "I didn't want to bother you," to which I politely respond, "I'll never know because you don't show." They don't go around with their heads hanging down. They just continue to do. Even when they want to quit, they understand the importance of foundations.

I would like to take the time to personally apologize to anyone in this group who may have felt overlooked, under-valued and ignored. You don't have to be a member of Point of Grace Ministries for me to apologize to you. Being in the body of Christ entitles and warrants one if that has occurred or currently may be happening.

PRAYER

Heavenly Father, Your word says in Isaiah 64:8
But now, O Lord, thou art our father;
we are the clay, and thou our potter; and
we all are the work of thy hand.
I come before You today thanking You for
revelation and understanding.
I thank You for wisdom for the journey and
the blessing of knowledge that I am
(INSERT THE STYLE OF SHEEP YOU CURRENTLY
ARE). *With this revelation, I yield myself over to the Holy*
Spirit to do as He pleases so You can get the glory out of my
life. Thank You for choosing me and loving me just as I am, yet
not letting me stay in this position. I give You praise for my
growth. I plead the blood of Jesus over my steps and my calling.
In Jesus Name, Amen

CHAPTER 9

————⬥•⬥————

SURELY GOODNESS & MERCY: A SHEPHERD'S SNARE

Many well-meaning sheep forget or are oblivious to the fact that pastors also have needs. *Then He returned to His disciples and found them sleeping. Couldn't you men keep watch with me for one hour?* (Matthew 26:40 NIV). Jesus, both Great Shepherd and meek Lamb, had need of intercession to continue in His purpose of redeeming the world from the grips of sin and death. His need was not directed to assist Divinity but instead to assist humanity. The God in Him was utilizing the Holy Spirit to make it possible to endure the cross, yet and still the man Jesus that walked, ate and slept with the disciples had a need.

One's purpose in life does not cancel personal needs. When

the shepherd lays in front of the sheepfold, it was not only to keep sheep in and the predators out, but it is also because the shepherd needed rest from his hard work in tending to the sheep. Devoted shepherds that have not adhered to *James 4:7 NIV Submit yourselves, then, to God. Resist the devil, and he will flee from you,* find themselves ill-equipped for the attack in which the enemy starts to run rough-shod in their lives. His purpose is to nullify the God given authority they possess even though they may not yet be utilizing it.

Many shepherds are busy doing ministry without submitting. Submission takes place through intimacy with God which enables them to hear and heed warnings from God. The enemy's desire is to sift us like wheat because if he can shake the shepherd's foundation, the sheep will scatter. Shepherds need to honest with themselves by acknowledging this fact: their calling does not make them exempt from struggles.

The prophet Elijah experienced one of his greatest natural struggles after one of his greatest spiritual victories. Those 450 false prophets of Baal were no match for the assigned prophet of God! Perhaps his mistake came with the mocking of the false prophets: *And it came to pass at noon, that*

> *His need was not directed to assist Divinity but instead to assist humanity. The God in Him was utilizing the Holy Spirit to make it possible to endure the cross, yet and still the man Jesus that walked, ate and slept with the disciples had a need.*

Elijah mocked them, and said, Cry aloud: for he is a god; either he is talking, or he is pursuing, or he is in a journey, or peradventure he sleepeth, and must be awaked (I Kings 18:27 NKJV).

It wasn't that he didn't win or wasn't destined to win, but his opponent studied him. The prophet Elijah was not unknown to the region. When we spend time in the presence of God, we are not an unknown in the kingdom of darkness. His victory caused the spirit of Jezebel to be stirred, so much so she sent warning that he would soon lose his life just as her false prophets had at Elijah's hand. This made the victorious prophet of God seek refuge in the wilderness. Fear, an all too human emotion, caused him to forget all about the victory God had just granted him, tuck tail, and run! Sadly a place of refuge was not satisfying enough. His next request to the Lord was for his own death. Fact, before Elijah began his journey of flight, he unintentionally spoke of his upcoming fate: *Then said Elijah unto the people, I, even I only, remain a prophet of the Lord. But Baal's prophets are four hundred and fifty men* (I Kings 18:24 NIV).

Mistakenly many shepherds have succumbed to the notion that they are the only one going through their particular issue. They unwittingly release their God given authority into the atmosphere speaking negative or defeating words, and creation starts to take place because it responds to our proclamations. Ezekiel was taken to a valley of dry bones and asked, *"Can the dry bones yet live?"* His response demanded creation to bow down to his voice. Elijah's proclamation summoned a spirit of death to come. I call these self-imposed limitations. "Self" brought it to fruition. "Self" needs to evict it. The ugly spirit of Jezebel said the next day she would have his life. The next day came and went and Elijah was still living. Shepherds need to recognize the spirit of isolation is usually, as in Elijah's case, fueled by intimidation and fear. It was fear sent to cause him to make rash decisions that sometimes were irrevocable in the natural and adhere in the spirit also.

Shepherds also need to avoid the tendency to take things personally when it comes to their relationship to sheep. When we reference Biblical sheep, to the untrained eye they may all resemble each other, but the owner of each pasture knows their sheep. I believe percentage of shepherds who experience burnout, discouragement and sometimes heartbreak and feel their only recourse is to leave the ministry is staggering. Unlike a secular job where you can leave your feelings at the office, shepherding is not conducive to leaving your heart in the church building.

Many years ago, I found myself spending a lot quality time with an individual in what I believed was spiritual mentorship. They depended on me for guidance, and I gladly shared the knowledge I had gained from my relationship with Christ and work in the ministry. Over time, however, I came to realize that the relationship was crossing boundaries. One day she told me how upset she was that I didn't respond to a particular situation the way she thought I would, and she was leaving the church.

Before I knew it, I was raising my voice trying to explain over her voice what was really going on. The Holy Spirit reminded me

> *His victory caused the spirit of Jezebel to be stirred, so much so she sent warning that he would soon lose his life just as her false prophets had at Elijah's hand. This made the victorious prophet of God seek refuge in the wilderness. Fear, an all too human emotion, caused him to forget all about the victory God had just granted him, tuck tail, and run! Sadly a place of refuge was not satisfying enough. His next pursuit was death.*

of how I encourage people all the time to take ownership for what they do, even if you feel it may cost you something. The release is payment enough. So I politely ended our heated dialogue with this declaration: *I will not take ownership for something I did not do. I know that I have done nothing wrong, so forgive me for your misunderstanding. I love you, but I will not carry this baggage.* My goal in that moment was to not allow a spirit of guilt, confusion, chaos, or manipulation to have the last word. Whether she knew it or not, the fact that my reaction to one incident was enough to cause her to leave the church indicated that there may have been a desire to leave just looking for the opportunity to do so.

The same concept can be applied to air travel. When you get on an airplane there is a specified baggage weight limit for carry on as well as checked bags. If your baggage exceeds the weight limit you must pay extra. Even if the passenger doesn't agree with the extra charges that are applied for multiple reasons, the baggage weight has a profound effect on more fuel being

> *I believe percentage of shepherds who experience burnout, discouragement and sometimes heartbreak and feel their only recourse is to leave the ministry is staggering. Unlike a secular job where you can leave your feelings at the office, shepherding is not conducive to leaving your heart in the church building.*

used. Most importantly, the added weight can lead to a safety hazard considering the fact that the aircraft was designed to carry a certain limit to its destination. This is the same in the spirit. If you intend to keep soaring in Christ, there must be a weight limit to the bags you are carrying. That means shepherds cannot carry or even handle all the bags that sheep may want to lay on them. Some bags (issues) are not really bags but strongholds and fortresses. This sometimes cannot be penetrated through normal interaction or intervention but may require deliverance.

I recently watched the broadcast of a well-known televangelist as he shared a captivating story of his visit to Jerusalem, about touring and observing three shepherds in their normal routine of taking their sheep to get water. What was so fascinating was the fact that all three groups of sheep mingled together on their quest to get water. They all drank from the same lake while the shepherds kept watch. He was so perplexed as to how the sheep would know which shepherd to follow as they prepared to leave the watering place! The pastor lingered around to see how this would play out.

To his amazement, after all three shepherds determined that the sheep had their share of water, each would make a sound and one by one he watched as the sheep separated from their drinking mate and followed the voice of their shepherd The sheep did not try to go to another field or listen to another shepherd. They instinctively returned to the one who fed, protected, groomed and would lay down his life for them. This is what Jesus was talking about when He said, *"The gatekeeper opens the gate for him, and the sheep listen to his voice. He calls His own sheep by name and leads them out"* (John 10:3 NIV).

The Lord said, *"And I will give you pastors according to mine heart, which shall feed you with knowledge and understanding"* (Jeremiah 3:15 NASB). Shepherds will hearken to the leading of the Lord on what to feed His sheep, knowing they belong to the Lord. Shepherds know the nutritional needs of the sheep more than the sheep. Being the mother of two, I know my children would have loved growing up in a house where they were allowed to eat whatever they wanted, whenever they wanted. Could you imagine your mother allowing you to have ice cream and soda for breakfast, lunch, and dinner? While this may sound preposterous, some pastors face what I call the attack of the "pleasing season." This is when messages are seasoned in sugar and the words amen, hallelujah and preach are more important than the content.

As a toddler my oldest son was a finicky eater. After he was weaned from the bottle, he refused to eat most of the foods I tried to give him. As the concerned new mother, I made an appointment with his pediatrician and explained all my concerns about how he just wouldn't eat. I just didn't know what else to do! His pediatrician leaned back in her chair and said with a beautiful yet firm smile on her face, "Mother, it takes over a dozen times to introduce a new taste to your child before he will accept it, so keep introducing it to him: eventually he will eat it." She rose to her feet proceeded to wash her hands which was a subtle way of informing me that our meeting was almost over.

> If you intend to keep soaring in Christ, there must be a weight limit to the bags you are carrying. That means shepherds cannot carry or even handle all the bags that sheep may want to lay on them. Some bags (issues) are not really bags but strongholds and fortresses.

She turned to me and said. "When he gets hungry enough, he will eat. You are a good mother. You won't let him starve. Remember, feed him what he needs, not always what he wants." I took that to heart so much so that when the next child came along 8 months later and started to exhibit those same unhealthy eating habits, I thought "Boy, you will starve so you better eat this food!" Fifteen years later, he is a healthy young man. God sent me to the right pediatrician who gave the right instructions, which leads me to the final snare set against shepherds.

The final snare to be mentioned is the snare that masquerades itself. Its intended victims do not recognize the effect until it has completed its task of destruction. Let's refer to the final snare as God's Property. Sheep/Parishioners/ Members - whatever term you are accustomed to using when referring to the people of God; they belong to God. The God's Property snare incorporates territorial, boundary, familiarity and soul issues.

I purposely saved this snare for last because it masquerades as if it is concerned, nurturing, or fulfilling an assignment. These are necessary qualifiers for the shepherd's role described by the prophet Jeremiah. Even with all of those qualities in place they don't discount the fact that sheep belong to God. He allows shepherds to lead them through a servant leadership lifestyle. Great leaders desire to comprehend their roles and fulfill their purpose. *"God said, Let us make man in our image after our likeness: and let them have dominion over the fish of the sea, and over the fowl of the air, and over the cattle, and over all the earth, and over every creeping thing that creepeth upon the earth"* (Genesis 1:28 NIV). The desirable likeness is that of the Trinity, Creator, Redeemer and Guide - not the leader's fleshly image.

Previously I shared the illustration of three shepherds who journeyed together as

> *Could you imagine your mother allowing you to have ice cream and soda for breakfast, lunch, and dinner? While this may sound preposterous, some pastors face what I call the attack of the "pleasing season." This is when messages are seasoned in sugar and the words amen, hallelujah and preach are more important than the content.*

they fed the sheep and how each sheep knew which voice to follow. Shepherds cannot get so territorial and possessive by not allowing the sheep to be sheep and graze, even if that means they eat in another field every now and then. I am by no means suggesting week after week, service after service grazing in another field as that classifies as a wandering spirit. Sadly enough there are shepherds that forbid sheep from visiting or fellowshipping anywhere outside of their place of worship. Shepherds cannot allow nurturing and protecting to cross over into manipulation or control. God doesn't manipulate at all and especially what already belongs to Him.

The word of God directs us to two significant women in the Bible who embody the mindset of "I belong to God." They are Mary and Hannah. Mary carried the Messiah with the knowledge that He would one day be the Savior of the world. At the appointed time Mary had to release the child Jesus into His God ordained purpose. He did not belong to her. Nevertheless, allowances come with restrictions. For instance, leaders should be held to a higher standard. If they say God has called them to a certain position, there must be an accountability factor that is adhered to. The answering of the call to lead requires their role to go beyond the role of lay members.

Boundaries are necessary for survival. Shepherds of old understood intentional separation for order to be present. Sheep were in close proximity to the shepherd, yet when it was time to rest there were no language barriers interfering with who goes where. God's word reveals shepherds and sheep spent a lot of time together. As a pastor, my style of delivering the word of God is to walk. I come from behind the pulpit and interact with the congregants. For a season, the Lord would not allow me to come off of the platform. It was quite uncomfortable because my nature is to connect through touch. Not physical touch but by getting close in proximity as to connect in the Spirit.

After I completed the assignment of being stationary on the platform, He added another twist. Sunday mornings, while the assigned minister taught our Christian education classes, I would remain in my office until the beginning of praise and worship and then come out of my office. This is not so that I could make a grand entrance, but I found that the alone time helped me clear my mind before delivering the Word. Since my personality is that of a greeter, people

> *Sadly enough there are shepherds that forbid sheep from visiting or fellowshipping anywhere outside of their place of worship. Shepherds cannot allow nurturing and protecting to cross over into manipulation or control. God doesn't manipulate at all and especially what already belongs to Him.*

want to hug, but for a season the Lord would not allow me to be touched before the service. The only way to protect this directive was to stay in my office until praise and worship was over. The separation was necessary in order to come before God's people without interference or distractions.

Then Samuel took the horn of oil and anointed him in the midst of his brothers, and the Spirit of the Lord came mightily upon David from that day forward. So, Samuel arose and went to Ramah (I Samuel 16:13 NASB). Scripture reveals that the prophet Samuel would not even get comfortable until the last of Jesse's sons were brought before him. Then the Word of the Lord revealed the king in their midst. David was anointed yet went back to his first assignment tending the sheep. The oil solidified the calling. Nowhere do we read that David was instructed that his time tending the sheep was over and not to go back. On the contrary, I believe it placed a seal on the shepherd's heart: a seal of humility to prepare him for the battles he would later encounter. Goliath was on the horizon. What the giant did not know was that the Anointing had already arrived!

David was a man after God's own heart. In spite all of his flaws and cover ups he still pursued a right relationship with God. The ability to approach the King comes when shepherds keep a watch over their hearts. Pastors are *gatekeepers* for a reason. That by no means gives them license to act indifferent or cold. On the contrary, what is needed is a discerning Spirit.

Shepherds are sent to help release keys. The key of authority is given to all Believers upon conversion but the understanding on how and which key to use is released through the sent one of God. *How then shall they call on Him in whom they have not believed? And how shall they believe in Him of whom they have not heard? And how shall they hear without a preacher?* (Romans 10:14 NIV). Shepherds are not the key, but their ordained assignments reveal the Great Shepherd to all who have an ear to hear.

Some time ago I went to visit a member of our church who was in the

> David was anointed yet went back to his first assignment tending the sheep. The oil solidified the calling. Nowhere do we read that David was instructed that his time tending the sheep was over and not to go back. On the contrary, I believe it placed a seal on the shepherd's heart: a seal of humility to prepare him for the battles he would later encounter. Goliath was on the horizon. What the giant did not know was that the Anointing had already arrived!

hospital. When I walked into the room another visitor was already there. I proceeded to sit and join in the conversation. Even though it was a visit that most pastors prefer not to make, it was enjoyable because the other visitor was quick witted with a great sense of humor. The topics of discussion jumped from family to church and everything in between. At one point in the visit, the nurse came in and asked us to step out for a moment while she attended to her patient.

When we walked back into the room, I received a formal introduction. The quick-witted visitor seemed amazed when she found out I was a pastor. She proceeded to tell me about all the churches she was affiliated with in the community. She shared with me that she left one church, joined another, and still had not found fulfillment . . .

Without asking her why she was still feeling empty, she stated, **"I became ill while attending both churches and ended up in the hospital and neither pastor came to visit."** It just so happened I knew both pastors and what she desired was not the culture in either church. My response was not to tell her she was wrong but to explain to her love languages of shepherds. It took some convincing for her to understand that my appearance that day did not make me more loving or sympathetic. I just knew the love language of the member I was visiting, and my appearance spoke to her love language. I reminded her in all honesty the Shepherds are to train the sheep to visit the sick. But that is for another book. On to Languages of love.

CHAPTER 10

---◆◆◆---

HE RESTORETH MY SOUL: LOVE LANGUAGES OF A SHEPHERD

Five Languages of Love:
Gifts, Affirmation, Transformational Changes,
Commitment, Unity in the Body

Being able to ascertain the language of love of your pastor does not require an intimate connection. However, it does require being intentional in loving them in their language, not yours. Expressing love to your pastor does not necessarily guarantee an intimate relationship. There should never be a hidden agenda for expressing love to your pastor. If there is, then the "love" is not real.

In ministry there are comrades or confidants which both

serve a purpose. Knowing which group you are in is crucial to thriving and not just surviving. Comrades are fellow soldiers that have common goals and interests. Their goal is not just having a personal connection. Comrades will continue to walk or work together to fulfill the will of the Father. Many comrades are seasonal and if there is a specific assignment, many times they might leave after it is completed.

Confidants on the other hand are not only able to meet shepherds at their love style, but they go beyond the outer court in the relationship. A confidant is trustworthy and may be privy to the private side of the shepherd. *"And it came to pass, when he had made an end of speaking unto Saul, that the soul of Jonathan was knit with the soul of David, and Jonathan loved him as his own soul"* (1 Samuel 18:1 NKJV). Confidants are usually more of a lifetime appointment. Even if they don't stay physically connected, this relationship may have generational affects (i.e., protection, intercession and commitment).

Gifts

Gifts come in a broad spectrum from a shirt and tie to automobiles. I can recall stories of my mother reminiscing about her childhood and how the families in the church would prepare meals for the pastors whether they were traveling preachers or stationary pastors. The language of love was a hearty home cooked meal. They made sure they did not go away empty handed and the meals were priceless. One should never be afraid to give gifts to the shepherd just because of the price tag (i.e., the widow's mite was more heartfelt and honored by God than all others).

Affirmation

Affirmation is emotional support where simple acts of encouragement are uplifting. Encouraging smiles and "Amen" every now and then can be enough to make a pastor's day. Let us not forget that occasionally the encourager needs encouragement. Shepherds are under constant attacks and it must be remembered that they are not infallible.

For this reason, it is a disservice to the pastor to be unwittingly exalted above God. Since the mind is usually the target of the attacks, kind words soothe soulish mind attacks. I once had a member make an appointment with me to discuss issues that were plaguing her family. Upon completion of our meeting, she asked what she could do for me. It was a heartfelt question that was released through genuine love and concern for me and my family.

Transformational Changes

Therefore, my beloved brethren, be ye steadfast, immovable always abounding in the work of the Lord, forasmuch as ye know that your labor is not in vain (1 Corinthians 15:58 NASB). There is very little that can be more rewarding than knowing that one's studying, teaching, equipping and sacrificing for others are enlarging the Kingdom of God and defeating the kingdom of darkness. Having the privilege to witness those whom you share the gospel grow in their God ordained purpose is not only exhilarating but fulfilling. A transformed life is that light that cannot be hidden which shines in this darkened world.

Commitment

The silent expression of love is an interpretation of commitment. It has been said that no one can be a leader if no one is following. It is a blessing to have others see and follow the God in you. Shepherds should never forget being chosen is an honor. I remember a well-known televangelist say that he once prayed to God to have fifty faithful members, not knowing that it would take five hundred to make fifty faithful. Commitment is supporting through your presence. So when the sheep fight to overcome the temptation to forsake the assembly of themselves, it is encouraging to the Shepherd.

Unity in the Body

Unity creates an atmosphere for the manifestation of signs and wonders. The purpose of the church is to bring the kingdom of heaven to earth. God has done His part, now it is time for us to do ours. He endued us with power and authority. Even though we know greater works shall we do, unity must be present to complete each assignment. Shepherds don't want the sheep to receive partial healing or partial deliverance or partial salvation. Unity solidifies the body, closes gaps and defeats schisms sent by the enemy.

I WILL DWELL: PRACTICAL WAYS TO ENCOURAGE YOUR PASTOR

The following are some suggestions. Seek the Holy Spirit for guidance and you will never go wrong.

1. Through your involvement in the church (never be just a spectator).

2. Pray for every facet of their lives always (i.e. spiritual, physical, financial, vocational, etc.).

3. With sensitivity to their schedule and the leading of the Holy Spirit, call them periodically just to see how they are doing and tell them that you love them.

   CAUTION: Do not unload your "troubles" and limit your call to 5-10 minutes.

4. Do not stand for anyone criticizing or bad-mouthing your Pastors. Stand up for your Pastors when they are not present to defend themselves.

5. Nurture your relationship with God without being totally dependent on the Pastors for your spirituality.

6. Encourage your Pastors with words and/or notes.

7. Never write "critical" letters to your Pastors, if there is a problem, it should be communicated face-to-face and very soon.

8. Gifts (as led by the Holy Spirit).

9. Monetary gifts, restaurant gift cards [enough for their family], a carwash, prepare a meal [if you know their likes and dislikes] and deliver to their home.

10. Respect their privacy, personal and family time (i.e. don't call & interrupt family dinner, etc.)

FROM THE HEART OF A SHEPHERD: A CLOSING NOTE OF LOVE

First of all, I want to thank you for supporting this vision by reading this book regardless of how you received it. Whether it was a gift, if you purchased it, or found it lying on the street corner, I'm glad it fell into your hands. Know that *I know* this is not an exhaustive discussion of any of the topics covered in this volume. There are many, many, many more words that could be written and probably should be. I just wanted to share a portion of what I've learned from observation, from experience, and from what the Lord has revealed to me through his Holy Spirit.

I don't know where you fall in the pages of this book. Are you a shepherd? A needy sheep? A dedicated one? Wherever you see yourself, I pray that God works through the pages of this book and causes the words you read to strengthen, to encourage, to deliver, to set free. I pray God's richest and most abundant blessings on you as you go forward.

I also pray you have found a place where your soul can

grow and the church or ministry where you feel connected. But if you have not, I encourage you to keep seeking God has a place for you. When you find it, you'll know it just like you know your name. It will fit you like a well-worn jacket or winter coat that you hate to let go because although it maybe threadbare, it is still comfortable to you. It is the place where you will learn to trust God more and more . . . and you will know that you are loved.

Printed in the United States
By Bookmasters